## PRAISE FOR *GAME CHANGERS: LEADING TODAY'S LEARNING FOR TOMORROW'S WORLD* **AND THE AUTHORS**

'Just what the world needs, huh? Another book about the need to radically transform education. But this is no dry academic treatise because Phil and Adriano have brought the same freshness to the task in hand that they adopted in their *Game Changers* podcast – lively, respectful and intensely practical. They have cleverly mined the gems of their guests' collective wisdom and drawn a compelling narrative that provides a manifesto for change, not just in Australia, but globally. If you're a school leader, you really do need this book – it will persuade, inform and practically demonstrate how you can create a school that's fit for the future.' – David Price OBE, author of *Open: How We'll Work, Live and Learn in the Future* and *The Power of Us: How We Connect, Act and Innovate Together*

'We must evolve how we lead to support young people to navigate the uncharted challenges of the twenty-first century. This book is jam-packed with essential wisdom about being the game-changing leader the world needs, orientating future generations towards a brighter and more compassionate future.' – Yasmin Poole, youth advocate, Rhodes Scholar and The King Center 2021 Youth Influencer of the Year

'Game changers see the emerging future and change the rules of the game or the game itself. In education, this is sorely needed if we are to create thriving societies and have a flourishing planet. This book by Phil and Adriano takes us deep into the mind, heart, character and being of a game changer. It shows us how they are creating schools of tomorrow with their vision, imagination and care for every child. The authors have brought together critical insights and strategies to help us create future-fit education ecosystems and transform societies where every child is thriving. If you want to create a school for tomorrow that has character, competency and wellness at its core, I invite you to read this book.' – Vishal Talreja, co-founder and trustee of Dream a Dream

'Education needs transformation. Small improvements cannot create the schools we need for tomorrow's world. Phil and Adriano present a wonderful book for school leaders who wish to lead the transformation.' – Yong Zhao, distinguished professor in the school of education at the University of Kansas and professor in the graduate school of education at the University of Melbourne

'In these times of societal and environmental collapse we have a choice to make between fear and hope. *Game Changers* has become one of my favourite sources of the latter. Phil and Adriano are uniquely positioned to help us grasp the "why", the "what" and the "how" of the leadership roles we are to step into if we are to develop with our young people a fighting chance to survive, thrive in and create a radically better world.' – Santiago Rincón-Gallardo, author of *Liberating Learning: Educational Change as Social Movement*

'This book makes a major contribution because it takes the agenda for the transformation of education one stage further and really lays out with forensic clarity the nature of the leadership that this task will require.' – Valerie Hannon, co-founder of the Innovation Unit and co-author of *Thrive: The Purpose of Schools in a Changing World*

'We keep saying that the time for change is now, and it is. But how many of us are truly courageous enough to do what needs to be done, to make the tough decisions, to transform schools and school leadership for young people and their world – as it is now (and is likely to become), not how it was? The work is hard, the challenge is significant, but together we can make a difference and "change the game". It's easy to talk about change; it's much more difficult to make it happen. That is how books like *Game Changers: Leading Today's Learning for Tomorrow's World* can help us progress. Grounded in evidence, supported by rich insights from practitioners from around the world and driven by a desire to be practical, this has the potential to become a text that educators actually read, not just add to the library and hope.' – Nathan Chisholm, principal of Prahran High School

'*Game Changers* is the thought leadership educators worldwide have been craving since Sir Ken Robinson told us education needs to be transformed. Phil and Adriano have taken that idea and run with it, providing a playbook for the next decade and beyond with the strategy and tactics to help your students flourish.' – Lacey Filipich, award-winning author, financial educator and founder of Money School

'In this inspirational book, Dr Phil Cummins and Adriano Di Prato propose a world where human-centred leadership shows its wholehearted self within the complexity of leading future-fit education. The depth and detail of their game changer approach reflects their keen observations and research, and provides a model of reflection and discovery all leaders would benefit from immensely.' – Tracey Ezard, keynote speaker, educator and author of *Ferocious Warmth: School Leaders Who Inspire and Transform*

'Phil and Adriano capture so much of what is required of leaders in this liminal time for schools and education. At a moment when so much is in flux, educational leaders need new skills, new literacies and, maybe most importantly, a different set of dispositions to effectively lead their communities into a future that is increasingly complex. *Game Changers* does a great job of clarifying what leaders must now become and, importantly, ways that they can begin their own personal transformations in earnest.' – Will Richardson, co-founder of the Big Questions Institute

'From the pages of this beautifully designed book, an intriguing and compelling leadership model emerges. Phil and Adriano are powerful voices in a growing community of educators who recognise that our school systems, success metrics and learning outcomes are increasingly out of tune with the demands and requirements of our world today. Like choirmasters in the pursuit of harmony, their wonderful *Game Changers* podcast brings together an eclectic mix of individuals who are challenging the status quo. The conversations they are conducting really matter, and by distilling key insights from leading changemakers into their book, Phil and Adriano have crafted, in the most human of ways, a list of leadership behaviours that will encourage and empower anyone facing up to the challenge of changing school.' – Cameron Fox, founding head of school, VERSO International School

PHILIP CUMMINS & ADRIANO DI PRATO

# GAME CHANGERS
## LEADING TODAY'S LEARNING FOR TOMORROW'S WORLD

The Game Changers brand logo has been designed by Tyron Tran trading under the name T7 and Copyright ownership rights remain the property of Philip SA Cummins and Adriano Di Prato.

© 2023 Philip SA Cummins and Adriano Di Prato

All rights reserved. No part of this book may be reproduced or transmitted in any form or by any means, electronic or mechanical, including photocopying, recording or by any information storage and retrieval system, without prior permission in writing from the publisher.

Published in 2023 by Amba Press, Melbourne, Australia.
www.ambapress.com.au

Previously published in 2022 by Hawker Brownlow Education.
This edition replaces all previous editions.

Editor: Lauren Mitchell
Designer: Matthew Harrod

ISBN: 9781923116108 (pbk)
ISBN: 9781923116115 (ebk)

A catalogue record for this book is available from the National Library of Australia.

# ACKNOWLEDGEMENTS

Writing a book can be as hard as it is rewarding. We wish to note that we would have been unable to complete *Game Changers: Leading Today's Learning for Tomorrow's World* without the support, positive contribution and guidance of many individuals and groups.

We wish to thank our awesome team at a School for tomorrow. Thank you to Kyle Porter for all his tireless work in securing our guest line-up for each series, to Matthew Donlon who supports each series by creating time for us to record and securing sponsorship, and to our producer, Oliver Cummins, for making us and our guests sound great!

Next we wish to thank everyone on the Hawker Brownlow Education team who helped us so much. Special thanks to Olivia Tolich, our ever-patient publishing manager who started the journey of this book with us, Lauren Mitchell, our super attentive and generous editor, and the entire design team for enhancing our words with their visual magic.

Thank you to Adriano's former VCE visual communication design student Tyron Tran for designing our playful and vibrant Game Changers brand logo.

Last of all, we wish to thank two groups. Firstly, thank you to our brave pioneers, our *Game Changers* podcast guests, who have brought so much of themselves and their lived experiences to each rich and deeply insightful conversation. And, finally, a massive thank you to our amazing *Game Changers* audience, an ever-growing group of people, each committed to changing the game in school and society.

### Personal note from Phil

I'm very grateful for all those who have taught me what I know about leadership over the course of a career and a life: family, friends, colleagues, scholars, thinkers and (most of all) students. I wouldn't be anywhere, let alone in a position to contribute to a work like this and pass on what I have learned, if it wasn't for the sacrifices my parents made and the strong value they placed on education being key to my or anyone's future. And thank you especially to Adriano for all that we have been able to do as a team in this and our broader enterprise.

### Personal note from Adriano

I wish to thank my mother, Hermine, and my late father, Antonio. Mum, an immigrant from Vienna, Austria, and Dad from Popoli, Italy, who both took the courageous step to travel a vast distance to a foreign country, very different to what was familiar, to create a new life for themselves and then subsequently our family. Their story, like that of many immigrant stories, is one of hard work, hope and optimism, stories that fundamentally changed the game in Australia, positively impacting on society, economics and culture. Their example, and the immigrant stories of so many, continues to inspire me today.

Thank you to my co-author and *Game Changers* co-host, Dr Philip SA Cummins. Phil initiated a phone call in early 2020 that has since yielded a dynamic and diverse podcast that influences thought and practice, and a global educational and leadership consultancy in a School for tomorrow that supports others to ultimately thrive. What a ride to date! Thanks *amico*.

Next I wish to acknowledge all the individuals I have had the opportunity to lead, be led by, or watch their leadership from afar – former students, colleagues and many wonderful friends. I want to say thank you for being the inspiration and foundation for *Game Changers: Leading Today's Learning for Tomorrow's World*.

And finally I dedicate this book to all the students I have had the privilege of teaching and leading over my entire educational career. Young people are remarkable and they continue to inspire me to be better than I was yesterday. Always remember that you matter, that you are enough and that permission is triumph.

# TABLE OF CONTENTS

Acknowledgements .................................................. vii

About the authors .................................................. xi

Preface ............................................................ xiii

Foreword by Valerie Hannon ....................................... xv

Prologue ............................................................ 1

Chapter 1: Leadership from the inside out .................. 21

Chapter 2: Leadership that strengthens .................... 45

Chapter 3: Leadership that informs ........................ 65

Chapter 4: Leadership that orientates ..................... 85

Chapter 5: Leadership that focuses ....................... 109

Chapter 6: Leadership that aligns ......................... 131

Chapter 7: Leadership that enriches ...................... 155

Epilogue .......................................................... 179

References ....................................................... 201

Index ............................................................. 207

# ABOUT THE AUTHORS

### Dr Philip SA Cummins FRSA FACEL FIML

**Phil** is an educator by trade and conviction. He is a co-founder and managing partner of a School for tomorrow.; the founder and managing director of CIRCLE – The Centre for Innovation, Research, Creativity and Leadership in Education; co-founder and head of education at Voyage; and associate professor of education and enterprise at Alphacrucis University College.

For over three decades, Phil has been teaching, thinking, writing, speaking and leading in schools and tertiary institutions all over the world. He began his career teaching history and Latin, and enjoyed coaching debating, cricket and rugby. He originally qualified in law and history, and his PhD focuses on the ANZAC myth and its cultural impact on Australian identity. He was commissioned as an officer in the Royal Australian Artillery and has served on the executive of a variety of professional and not-for-profit boards and consultative groups over the years. Phil is the author of more than twenty-five books and has published scholarly works, professional articles, poetry and plays in a variety of different contexts.

Now, as an entrepreneur, academic, researcher and consultant, Phil is acknowledged as a global leader in character education. He collaborates with thousands of colleagues, schools and other organisations who share a commitment to excellence and believe that 'character is the reason why we do school; it's the whole work of a school'. Phil's other areas of expertise concentrate on strategy, leadership, governance, educational design and high-performance learning. His work promotes the voice, agency and advocacy of students through purpose-driven, future-ready and future-fit schools. His opinion on education is sought by both government and media. He co-hosts the *Game Changers* podcast, an ongoing public education program with over 300 000 episode listens that celebrates outstanding examples of pioneering leadership in education and industry. He is a member of a range of professional associations and has been awarded fellowships by the Royal Society of the Arts, the Australian Council for Educational Leadership, and the Institute of Managers and Leaders.

The father of three adult children, Phil now lives in Fitzroy, Melbourne. He loves his family, cooking, music and the long line of rescue dogs who have blessed his life with loyalty and companionship since he was a boy.

### Adriano Di Prato

**Adriano** is a co-founder of a School for tomorrow., a globally recognised educational network supporting students, teachers and school leaders to thrive in our new world. Prior to this, Adriano was deputy principal at Marcellin College, Bulleen, for twelve years, where he was heralded for positioning the school as one of the best performing independent Catholic boys' schools in the state. He was deputy principal at Caroline Chisholm Catholic College, Braybrook, for four years. He has also held significant curriculum leadership roles (head of visual arts), operational roles (head of campus and college timetabler) and student wellbeing roles (year-level coordinator).

In March 2020, Adriano launched a new podcast – *Game Changers* – with co-host associate professor of education and enterprise Dr Phil Cummins. *Listen Notes* ranked *Game Changers* in the top 2.5 per cent most popular shows out of 2 859 743 podcasts globally, making it one of Australia's leading educational podcasts.

Adriano is a former president of the Victorian Catholic Secondary Schools Deputy Principals Association (VCSSDPA). He was on the VCSSDPA executive for ten years and in 2015 was awarded life membership (honorary) by the VCSSDPA for significant contributions to Catholic education.

Adriano's broad academic scholarship includes a Bachelor of Arts (Design) from Monash University; a Graduate Diploma in Education and a Master of School Leadership, both from the University of Melbourne; and a Graduate Certificate in the Management of Not-for-Profit Organisations from the Australian Catholic University (ACU). In 2017 he completed a theology study audit at ACU's campus in Rome, Italy. He is a current member of the Australian College of Educators.

In 2019, 2020 and 2021 he was honoured to be selected on the annual Hot List of movers and shakers in Australian education by *The Educator* magazine. In 2022 Adriano was listed in *The Educator*'s inaugural list of the fifty Most Influential Educators across the entire Australian education sector.

# PREFACE

We live in a rapidly changing world. Everyday life means living through complexity, being ready for the things that life throws at us and enjoying the good fortune with which we are blessed. There is a volume, pace and intensity to our times that mean we need to be in a position to respond to change readily and willingly. This means that all of us need to be able to muster our dispositions, capacity and the whole of our being to meet these challenges and to make the most of the opportunities that are presented to us.

This is the landscape of our world today; this is the context in which all of our schools are operating. We know that the old model for school is broken, despite the efforts of all of those in education who give their all to the students in their care. We know we need a new way of thinking about and doing school so that we are genuinely creating today's learning for tomorrow's world. We need to place humanity at the centre of what we do and use wellness by design to equip, empower and enable our people to flourish in their world. We need to build a school for tomorrow.

A school for tomorrow is equipped with education, culture, leadership and performance. These elements develop the character, competencies and wellness that empower students on The Pathway to Excellence, which in turn sees them acquire the adaptive expertise and self-efficacy required to thrive in our world. Educators in this community of inquiry and practice are informed by 'The Way', which we will discuss in detail in Chapter 1, and led by what we call game changers.

Game changers in education are those brave pioneers whose innovative ideas are shaping the landscape of future-fit schooling. They don't wait for permission. They are courageous enough in their leadership to make real change in their learning communities as they foster the growth of each young person in their care.

This book is designed to help you to think about the why, the how and the what of becoming a game changer. We propose a model for the character of game-changing leadership in schools that builds on our global educational research and incorporates insights from the *Game Changers* podcast. We will take you on a personal journey of discovery that is designed to equip, empower and enable you to change the game of school through leadership that strengthens, informs, orientates, focuses, aligns and enriches. We want to provoke your thoughts and reflection. We want you to commit to leading today's learning for tomorrow's world in the pursuit of a school for tomorrow.

Are you ready to join us on our adventure?

Let's go!

**Phil and Adriano**

# FOREWORD

Do we need another book about change in education?

Absolutely we do; and specifically, we need this book. I am delighted to offer a foreword to *Game Changers* for a number of reasons. The first is that we are not just talking about change. Every 'reform' movement of the last thirty years has been predicated on the need for change. Yet we remain tethered to what is fundamentally the model of schooling of a very different era. We have to be a lot clearer about the nature of the change that is now urgently required. At the heart of it is a new debate about purpose. What Phil Cummins and Adriano Di Prato have done with this work is identify with great power and specificity the nature of the transformation that the circumstances of humanity, and of our planet, now require.

Gradually, intergovernmental agencies are becoming aware of the magnitude of the task – a far more challenging one than the United Nations (UN) Sustainable Development Goal for education indicates. In September 2022, for the first time, the UN convened the Transforming Education Summit alongside its General Assembly, and in doing so sketched out the formidable agenda that confronts us if we are to develop a new paradigm for mass learning that is adequate to the times. Unfortunately, educational transformation is somewhat like the climate crisis (and of course they are linked) in that government representatives attending such global gatherings often align themselves to the cause in high rhetoric. But when they return to home turf, their commitments tend to evaporate.

I need not rehearse here the reasons why this work of transformation is urgent, inspiring and actually humanity's only hope. Phil and Adriano do that work and contribute to the fast-growing chorus of educators and concerned citizens around the world who are calling this out. But this book makes a major contribution because it takes the agenda one stage further, and really lays out with forensic clarity the nature of the leadership that this task will require – specifically, leadership of the institutions still known as *schools*, which must become very different organisations to the ones we are all so familiar with. For all the talk about building the demand for a new model of learning, creating a movement, empowering learners – all of which is, of course, relevant and important – nothing will happen without the right leadership.

This book goes a very long way, I believe, not just in describing what such leadership looks like, but also in providing much more. It creates a playbook, yes, but also a kind of companion. This companion will help leaders be honest with themselves; it will challenge and provoke them. But it will be their friend – because it acknowledges both the difficulty of the journey, but also the brilliance of the destination. This book makes a fine bridge between scholarship already existing in the field and the writers' own more experiential insights derived from sampling their research with living game changers. Readers will find suggestions and perspectives that are grounded in the work of educators who are struggling with this challenge right now. But the book remains conceptually coherent – readers will be able to navigate their way with the help of an overarching frame that makes sense. It combines rigour (discipline, analysis) with the sheer poetry of this calling – as they put it, 'the grace of being in the world'.

While having dedicated this book (and their previous work) to creating game changers, Phil and Adriano are, of course, themselves changing the game. And though it may be a cool metaphor, this is no game. Unless we succeed in redesigning education systems to empower young people to shape a very different future, it is absolutely no exaggeration to say that humanity is lost. It takes boldness and courage to take that on as a leader: to self-identify as one committed to a different educational agenda – even while necessarily satisfying some of the requirements of the old system. There is an urgent need for guides and supports for these courageous leaders. They will find them in this book.

Valerie Hannon

# PROLOGUE
## Changing the game of school

We believe that the old model of schooling is broken. We believe that it's time for game changers everywhere to show the way forward, to be bold pioneers who don't wait for permission. We believe that to do this we need to be leaders who model today's learning for tomorrow's world, scaffold a better way to prepare students to learn, live, lead and work, and coach others in how they might locate their purpose with their practice and align it with their people, place and planet.

In this prologue, we set up this book's central provocations: the global challenges in education today, the need for a new social contract in education and the nature of game-changing leadership in schools. We also introduce its structure and premise, blending educational research with wisdom and experiences in the field as told by guests of our *Game Changers* podcast.

### Education at a tipping point

What a time to be an educational leader! Educational systems all over the world, including our own here in Australia, have witnessed the decline of a model for schooling created over a century ago for yesterday's world. Students everywhere experience a static curriculum taught at a standardised pace by one teacher teaching one subject at a time. This may have worked well for an earlier context in which the social contract for education prepared generations of young people for productive citizenship in an industrialising society. In the decades leading up to 2022, the time of this book's publication, our context changed – and the powerfully disruptive era of COVID-19 has accelerated this process.

The world now works differently. Improved productivity has been enabled by technology that changes the scale, dimensions and connectivity of everything we do. Advances in artificial intelligence and automation continue to transform our local, regional and global economies. People need to do different work to contribute effectively and be remunerated appropriately.

This reality brings with it massive implications for leaders across all sectors of education. As Professor Mark Hutchinson, vice president of development and professor of history at Alphacrucis University College, New South Wales, argues, schools still have a unique case to argue for their social function so long as they retain their relevance in a fast-moving world.

## GAME CHANGER INSIGHT

*'Schools are incredibly important social institutions for the leverage that they provide on bringing about adaptation to social change and helping families engage with their communities ... Yet, most schools are looking at a massive disconnect in their classrooms with disinterested students who can no longer simply be punished into compliance ... Students need to be able to expect that there's going to be an individualised approach to engaging them, educating them and directing them and providing opportunities for them in the areas which they find engaging and fulfilling.'*

**Professor Mark Hutchinson**

We are at a crossroads. Educational leaders can't sit back and wait for evolution to happen to us. To create change, school leaders must do something to transform schooling to then support the transformation of the rest of society. Action is essential. The transformation of our education systems needs to be led by game-changing educational leaders who imagine paths forward to futures that most cannot see, co-design new learning models to engage communities in powerful narratives of transformation and lead necessary changes across the field of education to create future-fit ecosystems.

The World Economic Forum (2020) identifies eight critical characteristics of high-quality learning in the age of the fourth industrial revolution – 'Education 4.0' – to shift learning towards the needs of the future:

1. *Global citizenship skills: Include content that focuses on building awareness about the wider world, sustainability and playing an active role in the global community.*
2. *Innovation and creativity skills: Include content that fosters skills required for innovation, including complex problem-solving, analytical thinking, creativity and systems analysis.*
3. *Technology skills: Include content that is based on developing digital skills, including programming, digital responsibility and the use of technology.*
4. *Interpersonal skills: Include content that focuses on interpersonal emotional intelligence, including empathy, cooperation, negotiation, leadership and social awareness.*
5. *Personalized and self-paced learning: Move from a system where learning is standardized, to one based on the diverse individual needs of each learner, and flexible enough to enable each learner to progress at their own pace.*
6. *Accessible and inclusive learning: Move from a system where learning is confined to those with access to school buildings to one in which everyone has access to learning and is therefore inclusive.*
7. *Problem-based and collaborative learning: Move from process-based to project- and problem-based content delivery, requiring peer collaboration and more closely mirroring the future of work.*
8. *Lifelong and student-driven learning: Move from a system where learning and skilling decrease over one's lifespan to one where everyone continuously improves on existing skills and acquires new ones based on their individual needs. (p. 4)*

Source: World Economic Forum. (2020, January 14). Schools of the Future: Defining New Models of Education for the Fourth Industrial Revolution. www.weforum.org/reports/schools-of-the-future-defining-new-models-of-education-for-the-fourth-industrial-revolution/ Attribution-NonCommercial-NoDerivatives 4.0 International https://creativecommons.org/licenses/by-nc-nd/4.0/

In many ways, these eight critical characteristics define the nature of the adaptive expertise and self-efficacy that might arise from active learning experiences in an education. This experience must be purposeful in its design and implementation of a scope and sequence of real-world opportunities for the transfer of foundational literacies, capabilities and dispositions that comprise the character and competencies required to thrive in a new world environment. They must also be grounded in strong foundations of wellness and be shaped by the fundamental understanding that all young people are home to a life.

Over the past decade, through our global network of a School for tomorrow. and its research institute CIRCLE – The Centre for Innovation, Research, Creativity and Leadership in Education, we have been engaged in a global research program about the character of an excellent education (read more at www.aschoolfortomorrow.com). We have found that parents and school communities everywhere want children to graduate from school with the integrity of character shown by good people; the leadership and communication of future builders; the change readiness and innovation of continuous learners and unlearners; the creative and critical thinking of solution architects; the perspective and balance of local, regional and global responsible citizens; and the inclusive collaboration skills and relationality of team creators. We will return to these graduate outcomes in 'Chapter 1: Leadership from the inside out'.

While our existing school systems have paid some attention to achieving these outcomes, our hardworking teachers have been left to fit them into a system that was never designed for this purpose. Too many of us in schools have been held back by system paralysis. Our days are too full. The requirements seem overwhelming. We are trying to fulfil expectations for tomorrow using yesterday's model. We end up educating without being able to truly feel for and respond to our new world environment.

At the same time, many of us can see through the challenges of the present day into a future where the possibility of something better is rapidly being drawn into sharp focus. Everyday life means navigating through complexity towards the future, being ready for the interruptions that are imposed on us and enjoying the good fortune with which we are blessed. The opportunity is there to do something great, if only we could all agree on what it is and how we might take that big step forward and up to make it happen.

Prior to 2020 we knew already that we were living in a moment of historic importance in education across the globe. No matter our individual appetite for change, if we were being honest with ourselves we knew that our schooling model had been designed for a different world and was no longer fit for purpose. We knew inside ourselves that we needed to be designing and delivering today's learning for tomorrow's world. And then the more immediate and exponentially fraught crisis of the COVID-19 pandemic began. UNICEF estimated in mid-2020 that the pandemic had impacted 1.6 billion children across the globe within the first few months of the crisis alone (UNICEF Data, n.d.). Suddenly, even describing the journey from yesterday to today to tomorrow became an unfamiliar and unpredictable daily struggle for many.

As a profession, we discovered new reserves of resilience and ingenuity. We learned and continue to learn so much about the capacity of our profession to respond to a crisis in a constructive and effective manner. Things that had eluded us for decades suddenly became possible because collectively we realised we had to make it work – and the more we adapted our practice to this purpose in support of our people and our place, the clearer it became that we could do what was required and more. More of our number began to ask the question 'What might happen if …?' as they began to adopt hitherto outlier dispositions towards innovation.

So, while thoughts, conversations and debates about educational transformation were occurring prior to the pandemic, 2020–2021 was a tipping point – not just for digital education, but for the entire education system. So much of what seemed impossible or undesirable at the start of the pandemic became first possible, then desirable and then necessary. Transformation was brought on by things both beyond and within our control.

Since February 2020, with the *Game Changers* podcast and also our consulting and research practice through a School for tomorrow., we have engaged in many rich conversations with teachers, social entrepreneurs, and business and educational leaders around the world about what is happening in education in response to the COVID-19 pandemic. What we have seen from students, teachers, leaders and teams in schools globally tells us so much about what we can do in education when we recognise the imperative to take a big step forward and up. This is not simply about a shift towards greater integration of technology in education, although that is certainly part of the answer. This is about recognising that educational leaders don't have to do things the way they have always been done.

From a situation that has arisen out of necessity, we have been changing. We have been taking away from our present experiences a set of new competencies. Our knowledge, skills, dispositions and learning habits are all changing because they must. Similarly, we have been asking serious questions about what might be a better way to create today's learning for tomorrow's world so that we can continue to model the character, competency and wellness we need to be producing with our students. Emerging from this is the growing realisation and corresponding acceptance that schooling as we once knew it is over.

We need a new way for today's children and the generations to follow. We need a different and better and future-fit way to prepare students to learn, live, lead and work. We need a new understanding of our purpose, our people, our place, our planet and our practice in education. We need to build the case for this approach to education globally.

We need to change the game of school.

## A new social contract for education: Today's learning for tomorrow's world

It is clear to us that it is time to frame a new approach to schooling that is truly today's learning for tomorrow's world. As Yong Zhao, distinguished professor in the School of Education at the University of Kansas and now also professor in the Graduate School of Education at the University of Melbourne, spells out, this approach must be both wholly human and responsive to the reality of our new world environment.

### GAME CHANGER INSIGHT

'I think the purpose of school is really to help every and each individual student discover and uncover their strength and passion, to help them expand that passion and their unique talents and then help them to find a way to turn their uniqueness into something that's valuable to others and to better the world. That's education, I think. But that is not normally shared because schools belong to different institutions, to different nations. I think a lot of time that we have overemphasised the role of the economy and of educating a workforce, but I think it's about humanity, the growth of individual human beings and treating ourselves as members of a global society that's connected.'

**Professor Yong Zhao**

The old story of grafting new ideas onto old structures doesn't work for us anymore. Our new story needs to be one of real and abiding change. Educational leaders need to identify those traditions and values that will stand us in good stead along the way, but also need to recognise that defaulting to the status quo means that we will be left behind. Our story must be premised on a better normal of continuous learning and therefore continuous growth. We need to change ourselves. We need to change our work. We need to change the way we connect with and support the whole of learning for our students and their families. We need to change the game of education right now.

Shifting our education system to meet the demands of our times will mean increasingly moving away from an industrial age, one-size-fits-all model in which teachers stand and deliver and learners sit and get. Teachers, leaders, schools and their communities must rethink conventional learning models and rapidly build, test and pilot new structures to accommodate a completely different reality. To accomplish the necessary shift in education for a world going through exponential change, educational leaders need to refocus and change the content of our goals beyond competitive targets, prime for clickbait, related to decontextualised, standardised testing. The system is not there to justify itself. As proclaimed by Valerie Hannon and Amelia Peterson (2021) in their seminal book *Thrive: The Purpose of Schools in a Changing World*, 'today, education has to be about learning to thrive in a transforming world' (p. xiv). It's there to bring people together in a community of inquiry and practice to improve the way every learner learns, lives, leads and works.

What might these improvements look like? We need to embrace the reality that our communities everywhere are changing and, ergo, so must we. This means becoming future focused, both by disposition and by nature. Tomorrow's world is becoming more highly personalised. Learning needs to anticipate and lead the way with this need for systems that are more human centred. We need to hardwire curiosity, creativity and ingenuity in everything we do (especially in incorporating technology to enhance learning outcomes), as well as the whole process of the transformation of the lives of our learners, for which we are stewards.

We need, then, to imagine what the models for schooling might look like within this new story that describes the fulfilment of this purpose for education. Andreas Schleicher (2020), director of the Organisation for Economic Co-operation and Development (OECD) Directorate for Education and Skills, has proposed four scenarios for what education might look like in 2040:

1. *Schooling extended*
*Participation in formal schooling continues to expand. International collaboration and technological advances support more individualised learning. The structures and processes of schooling remain.*

*2. Education outsourced*
*Traditional schooling systems break down as society becomes more directly involved in educating its citizens. Learning takes place through more diverse, privatised and flexible arrangements, with digital technology a key driver.*

*3. Schools as learning hubs*
*Schools remain, but diversity and experimentation have become the norm. Opening the 'school walls' connects schools to their communities, favouring ever-changing forms of learning, civic engagement and social innovation.*

*4. Learn-as-you-go*
*Education takes place everywhere, anytime. Distinctions between formal and formal and informal learning are no longer valid as society turns itself entirely to the power of the machine.*

*('Four scenarios for the future of schooling' section)*

Source: OECD/(Schleicher) (2020), (Future Proof? Four Scenarios for the Future of Schooling), https://oecdedutoday.com/future-proof-four-scenarios-future-schooling/.

If our role in schools is to prepare students to thrive in the new world environment, then we need educational leaders to be prepared to take and adapt ideas such as those proposed by Schleicher (and others) as we co-create our students' learning to allow them to articulate, reflect and explore the character, competency and wellness that we should be modelling, scaffolding and coaching for them.

Yet it goes beyond this. We need a new social contract for education: today's learning for tomorrow's world. We need to house this learning within an ecosystem that is human centred; technology enriched; people, place and planet conscious; and (above all) intentionally purposeful. We need to create schools that honour and manifest this new social contract for education by locating our purpose in our practice and propelling it forward to serve people, place and planet through our vocation.

This is our true calling, our vocation, our raison d'être as game changers: to create a school for tomorrow in and through which all might thrive.

This idea of a school for tomorrow is so important to us that we named our own global organisation after it! A school for tomorrow needs to be deeply imbued with an integrity of vision, strategy, operations and culture that is defined by the convergence of what it believes, what it aspires to and how it goes about what it does. It also needs a values and value proposition that shapes all of its aspirations, experiences and outputs in at least three fundamental ways.

In the first instance, the community of a school for tomorrow aspires to honour a shared commitment to a cause rooted in the compelling social rationale that its graduates should thrive by experiencing belonging, fulfilling their possibility and doing what is good and right in the world. From this, it crafts an educational purpose based on a shared perspective of the central importance of civic, performance and moral character through competencies that ask them deliberately and simultaneously to know, to do, to be and to learn, and also through the wellness that underpins them.

Secondly, a school for tomorrow plots an agreed organisational strategic trajectory for this work through its educational practice. This involves a deliberate, intentional and aligned operational process to design and deliver learning that allows students to reveal their character, demonstrate their competencies and experience wellness in a scope and sequence of learning experiences directed towards improving the frequency, rate, consistency and quality of the attainment of a set of agreed graduate outcomes.

Finally, a school for tomorrow goes about what it does by grounding meaningful, connected and integrated learning models and systems in a deep appreciation of people, place and planet. From this understanding of the context of schooling and the society it serves, a school for tomorrow propels forward the emerging voice, agency and advocacy of students on their pathway to adulthood. These students wrestle with what they think about their mark (their inner sense of fulfilment) and their measure (their sense of validation according to their capacity to cultivate and put into practice values, beliefs and actions associated with what others expect of them in terms of self-awareness, relationships, service and vocation). They apply this to how they learn, live, lead and work. As they grow through relationships of character apprenticeship and experiences of immersive learning, they acquire adaptive expertise and self-efficacy through their mastery of the graduate outcomes. In time, they also acquire the autonomy and purpose that allow them to reveal the manner in which they have grown as whole people who are ready to thrive in and contribute to their world.

And so, character, competency and wellness are the reason why we do school. They are the whole work of a school. Our research globally tells us that there are four understandings about the nature of this work that game-changing leaders need. They need to understand that character, competency and wellness are learned everywhere in a school. This learning occurs through a combination of specific pedagogies grounded in specific, designed relationships of character apprenticeship. Leaders are sustained by the curation of culture and supported by an evidence-based community of inquiry and practice that is focused on better outcomes for more learners.

This notion of improved outcomes for each and all is the expression of a robust and resilient culture of high-performance learning. This must be supported by an evidence-based and research-driven educational framework built and sustained by an authentic community of inquiry and practice. In this light, we need to recognise and educate students both for and in step with the holistic nature of the character, competency and wellness that most effectively express the best of humanity in our times. At the same time, the culture of high-performance learning integrates the essential content – the knowledge, skills, dispositions and learning habits – into learning that is explicit and implicit, and planned and spontaneous to build the capability of learners and graduates to express their emerging identities more completely and more vocationally in the world of tomorrow.

This takes more than just responding to the dictates of compliance. It takes educational leadership that is courageous and compassionate in its vision, bold and creative in its execution and game-changing in its impact.

## Leading as game changers

So, are we ready to be game changers who do this work? Are you ready to be a game changer? Ordinary people know their limits; bold and courageous educational leaders know how to push them. Game changers are brave pioneers who realise that it is time to stand up and celebrate our collective wisdom to transform learning and schooling as we know it. They don't ask permission; they step forward and up to transform their schools, their communities and their world. In his bestselling book *The Element: How Finding Your Passion Changes Everything*, Sir Ken Robinson (2009) stated:

> *The fact is that given the challenges we face, education doesn't need to be reformed – it needs to be transformed. The key to this transformation is not to standardize education but to personalize it, to build achievement on discovering the individual talents of each child, to put students in an environment where they want to learn and where they can naturally discover their true passions. (p. 376)*

Many educators felt instinctively that Robinson was right when he first made that statement over a decade ago. What we know now is that this act of transformation never stops. We don't do it once; we do it all the time by enlisting the voice, agency and advocacy of all our students, staff, families and communities to build the character, competency and wellness required to thrive in our world.

Game changers understand they have a responsibility to shepherd all in their learning community towards this shared goal. Global thought leader in education and co-author of *Thrive: The Purpose of Schools in a Changing World* Valerie Hannon offers a perspective on the exercise of leadership in this context that is very helpful.

> **GAME CHANGER INSIGHT**
>
> *'You know what great leaders do? Great leaders make great stories. They connect the dots. And I think that that's what the leaders of schools need to be doing.'*
>
> Valerie Hannon

It is in this way that game changers have a capacity for tuning in and outward. They can anticipate opportunities that are born of moments of real challenge, struggle, opportunity and celebration to take responsibility for the moral purpose of transforming schools. They do this most significantly through values, relationships and story.

If we are to be game changers who help their communities to write new stories together, we have some choices to make. First, we need to choose to go forward to help our schools become schools for tomorrow. We need to be disposed towards the future. We recognise that we don't have to go back to how things were. This doesn't mean throwing everything away. It does, however, mean that we, as educational leaders, must question what we do and make decisions to ensure that we are fit for purpose, that our vision matches our intentions and actions. We need to walk the walk of an education in which we cast aside broken models, adapt what we have left in place or retool from the ground up.

We need to honour the relevant legacy of yesterday, attend to the needs of today and build everything our schools do towards the tomorrow that their students will inhabit. We need to strive to be future fit with vision, vocabulary, and values and value propositions that speak to the new social contract of education: today's learning for tomorrow's world. We need to be committed to connecting students, teachers, leaders and school teams to these values and value propositions and the purpose of creating better outcomes for more learners so that they can grow, make progress and succeed on their pathway to excellence.

We also need to respond to our post-pandemic situation. This is about anticipating the opportunities that come from moments of real struggle and challenge. This is about developing a disposition towards improvement and an intention to make it happen. This is about designing a flexible, incremental and inexorable approach towards achieving better outcomes for more learners. This is about creating momentum and overcoming all obstacles through robustness and resilience when many in society are still frozen in an old reality.

As educators, we may not be able to see the future in entirety, nor can we hope to map out and control all the details. Nonetheless, it is clear to us that all educational leaders need to move forward and honour our responsibility to help the young people in our care to thrive in their world – for themselves, for the people around them and for all places across the globe. Together we can and should make that our difference.

We need to design a school for tomorrow intentionally so that it can build the character, competency and wellness that will allow students to thrive in their world. To create this whole education for a whole person we don't need to be perfect or even exceptional. We need to be committed to growth and to being the best version of ourselves so that our students can become the people they need to be. Educational leaders need to muster self-efficacy – how well we organise the dispositions and capacity of our whole being to meet our challenges. Educational leaders also need the adaptive expertise to make the most of the opportunities that are presented to us and create new solutions to our challenges.

This commitment to transformation and thriving calls on us to equip, empower and enable our students to demonstrate the graduate outcomes that communities all around the world want for their students. If we want students to be transformed, we need to choose to transform teachers and schools so that they can create the learning that models, scaffolds and coaches students towards success with the outcomes of thriving in a school for tomorrow. We know that it is the quality of teaching efficacy that makes the greatest difference in the outcomes of learners.

To transform student outcomes with a human-centred educational model that equips, empowers and enables those students to thrive and succeed in their world, educational leaders need to understand how to transform the learning of their teachers as much as the learning of their students. This also means we need to take on that combination of vulnerability and kindness that allows us to reveal who we are and who we are becoming, our authentic and best selves in service of our people, our place and our planet.

## A GAME-CHANGING APPROACH TO LEADERSHIP

Is there an approach to educational leadership that might help us to put our new social contract of today's learning for tomorrow's world in place? Leadership is the capacity to influence, inspire, direct and motivate people to achieve a shared sense of purpose willingly. We believe that there is an inside-out developmental process of leadership formation that can help you to ask and answer the most important questions about the character of game-changing leadership:

1. Who am I?
2. Where do I fit in?
3. How can I best serve others?
4. Whose am I?

As you craft and recraft responses to these questions throughout your career, you will gain adaptive expertise and self-efficacy, the concepts of self-awareness, relationship, service and vocation, and the expression of specific leadership competencies that will help you to influence, inspire, direct and motivate as you learn, live, lead and work in relationship with your communities of inquiry and practice.

You will also adopt and hone a set of capabilities of leadership in action through which you can seek to honour the new social contract of education by leading today's learning for tomorrow's world: strengthening, informing, orientating, focusing, aligning and enriching. In time, as you develop these capabilities, you will come to locate your purpose in your practice through your service to your people, place and planet. How you situate your leadership in action within its context and within relationships is key to your success as a game changer. As we look around the world and talk with students, teachers, leaders and school teams in our global a School for tomorrow. network, we can see that the very best schools are built on positive and collaborative relationships as well as the trust and confidence that emerge from them. This has much to do with the strongly relational personal qualities of many school leaders who are already game changers and their determination to lead by example in everything they do on at least four levels: personal, tactical, strategic and global.

You need to build relationships with individuals through your personal leadership. While many may have practised this craft significantly earlier in their careers and wish to spend more time in this dimension, the reality is that the greater the responsibility that you take on in a school, the greater the limits that will be imposed on your capacity to create meaningful and sustainable deep relationships with individuals. Most of us can only perform this mentoring or coaching role properly with a handful of people at any one time. It will be more effective, therefore, for you to build the majority of your individual relationships with the purpose of inspiring and motivating than trying to do the work of direction and influence by sitting beside people on a day-to-day basis.

The second dimension of relational leadership – how we build relationships with teams – is tactical. We have more opportunity to interact with a greater number of teams than ever before, but we probably can only allow ourselves to spend so much time with each group before we need to move on to another. As such, the energy and emotion of our role will often be dominated by enhancing teams' journeys through solving problems and making decisions, creating role-modelling culture and standards, building the capacity of team members to do their jobs and grow into their next roles, and engineering teamwide commitment to the strategy and operational effectiveness that will see it convert vision into reality.

Strategic leadership is the third dimension and pertains to how we apply ourselves to the challenges and choices of our organisation and also the direction in which it will need to travel to reach its preferred future. Again, we need to make wise choices about how we invest our time by focusing on those things that will make the greatest difference in the long run for our schools. As such, our aim needs to be to create a vision for the destination of our journeys and to help the organisation to align, implement and evaluate what our schools do to ensure the greatest positive impact on intention, design and culture.

The final dimension of relational leadership – global leadership – connects our school with its wider world. In this respect, we are building relationships with our schools' different and intersecting communities, negotiating and advocating for the place of the school and the value proposition it offers. In doing so, a game changer assists their school to define its preferred position and situate itself within its context by reinforcing its purpose, commitment and connections within the community.

All these dimensions of leadership have an impact on a leader's personal journey of discovery and the success of their school's journey. For it is leaders who show the way forward. They do the very important work of personalising, aligning and integrating the values and value propositions of an education for character, competency and wellness into a daily experience and supportive ecosystem that equips, empowers and enables students with the adaptive expertise and self-efficacy for them to experience growth, progress and success as they thrive in our world.

Educators around the world tell us that this means that leaders who are game changers need to learn about knowing right from wrong and having the courage to act. They need to understand how to create experiences that spark the joy of learning and the grace of being in the world. They need to help others to gain the satisfaction of getting the job done and doing it well. They need to know what it feels like to live in positive relationships and work with others well.

Game changers need to know these things because these are the experiences of the education in which we want our learners to share and grow. Our learners can learn much about ourselves from curriculum, content and process. Yet, most importantly, the formal and informal educational process of young people needs the presence of significant role models who can lead them through a process of character apprenticeship, from childhood to youth to adulthood, and support them to acquire that adaptive expertise and self-efficacy that evidences their capacity to thrive. In due course, these young people will take on learners as their own apprentices and then let them go to teach what they have learned to others. In this way, we all come to understand that it's about what we give – the things we pass on to others, the legacy we leave behind – that truly defines our best impact on the world as true servants and stewards of people, place and planet.

Of course, we will need to model the same character and processes that we expect of our students and colleagues. Only in this way will we be able to practise leadership by example. As leaders in relationships with others at personal, tactical, strategic and global levels, we model, scaffold and coach. We need to be living proof that it is worth taking the big step forward and up into today's learning for tomorrow's world through an ongoing process of building self-awareness, relationship, service and vocation through the inside-out process of development.

Thus, our own leadership character as game changers will be formed in much the same way as our learners' as we go about this work. All of us need to make our mark on the world by expressing our inner drive and we all want to measure up to the expectations of those around us. Just as our students will do, we will wrestle with these two concepts throughout our lives, finding authentic resolution and contentment in the understanding that a worthwhile life is spent placing the needs of others before ourselves.

## Getting the most out of this book

This book shows you how to lead as a game changer in a school for tomorrow. It shows you how and why schools need to meet the challenge of our times to equip, empower and enable young people to thrive in their world. It shows you how to bring a community of inquiry and practice together and lead it to create future-fit solutions that are evidence based and research driven.

Chapter 1 introduces the four-part developmental process of leadership formation (first noted on page 13), which asks:

1. Who am I?
2. Where do I fit in?
3. How can I best serve others?
4. Whose am I?

This first chapter helps you to think through this process and align its steps to the competencies of learning, living, leading and working that learners need to thrive in their world. Using the questions posed by the four-part developmental process of leadership formation, Chapters 2–7 support you to encounter, discover and explore each of the six identifiable capabilities of game-changing leadership required to inspire and support today's learning for tomorrow's world: strengthening, informing, orientating, focusing, aligning and enriching. Finally, the epilogue will help you to consider the 'secret sauce' of the character of game changers and put together all you have learned to create a model of your own leadership.

### Game changer insights

In this book we share our decade of extensive international research into game-changing leadership in education. We also share key learnings about leading from our encounters with over a hundred educational, societal and industry game changers who have featured on our *Game Changers* podcast since 2020. In fact, at this point in the prologue you'll have already come across a few.

Each game changer you hear from in this book is dedicating their vocation to meet the need for the new social contract of education. Each recognises that education has a much bigger role to play than simply equipping young people for the communities and the jobs of the future. Each leads by example in modelling the character and competencies of game-changing leadership.

### Encounter and respond

We believe making one's mindset the subject of conscious scrutiny is a prerequisite of being an effective, game-changing leader. Throughout each chapter you'll experience 'Encounter and respond' sections that will invite you to reflect on your existing thinking and practice. These simple activities are designed to help you grow and transform your leadership.

Taking time to slow down and reflect on your experiences is vital for improving your self-awareness and creating space for intention and improvement. We learn and grow from all our many and varied lived experiences. We see taking the time to consider these lessons as acts of self-care. Reflective practice accelerates improvement in your leadership skills and enables you to better understand yourself and the practice and performance of others.

When engaging with each invitation to encounter and respond consider these three tips:

1. Give yourself permission to narrate your experiences.

You may already identify as having a growth mindset or being a continuous learner and unlearner. Go one step further by making it explicit by creating space for reflection. Focus on getting all your thoughts, feelings and ideas down. Be as descriptive as possible in your writing. Schedule ten or thirty minutes a day (or week) into your calendar to protect the time for this reflection routine. Ideally, you'll set time aside to write every day; you may even choose to record you speaking instead. Whichever method you choose, just making time each week is a great start. Try to find a quiet time and place without distractions.

2. Be honest.

It's important to be realistic and acknowledge personal blind spots and weaknesses. This also means checking for unconscious bias and mining for the positive, which may be disguised as a learning opportunity. Challenge yourself to identify what went well, one strength you exercised or something you learned. Be solution focused; take the learning from any 'failures' and plan actions and a practice to improve. Finally, consider your responsibility and the consequences for your (in)action.

3. Collaborate with a peer, coach or mentor.

Find a peer to share experiences with on a regular basis. It could be someone at a similar level within your school or even someone operating in a similar role at another school. Make time to sit down and unpack recent experiences together, explore different options and ideas, and develop insights. Peers can add perspectives you hadn't considered.

## Let's go!

In short, we want to walk you through the way the character of game-changing leadership in our profession is being practised today. We will supplement our own research and understanding of the theory and practice of leadership centred on today's learning for tomorrow's world with the accounts of game changers in the field. We might even create some provocations and have a little fun along the way.

We invite you to take the big step forward and up to lead as game changers.

We're excited to go on this journey together.

We can't wait.

So, let's go!

# CHAPTER 1
## Leadership from the inside out

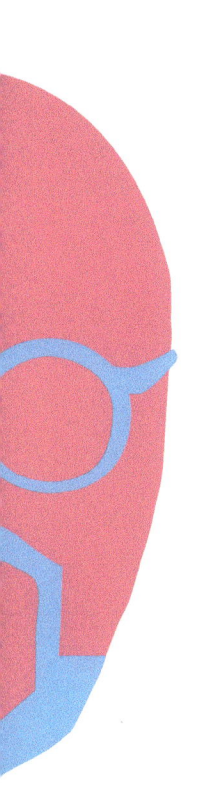

### THE CHARACTER OF GAME CHANGERS

At a School for tomorrow. we believe that when we reduce all of the process and practice of education to its essence, we reach a point where it's all about purpose: the purpose of learners, the purpose of teachers, the purpose of schools and the purpose of those who lead them. Game changers are those brave pioneers whose sense of purpose and innovative ideas are shaping the landscape of future-fit schooling. They don't wait for permission. They are courageous enough through their leadership to make real change in their learning communities. This change is directed towards fostering the wellness of each young person in their care so that they can build the necessary character and competency to thrive in our new world environment. To this end, within specifically designed relationships that we call *character apprenticeship*, game changers model, scaffold and coach for learners who articulate, reflect on and explore the adaptive expertise and self-efficacy required for them to experience growth, progress and success on their pathways to excellence.

Are you a game changer? Do you have the character of a game changer? What is your purpose as an educator and how do you intend to put it into practice? In the next six chapters of this book, we will use the prompts of game changers from around the world to help you to think through your purpose as an educator and how to put that purpose into practice through the six capabilities of leadership in action:

1. Leadership that strengthens – bringing the values and value of good people through your disciplined and purpose-driven practice.
2. Leadership that informs – sharing the compelling narrative of future builders through how you create and communicate vision.
3. Leadership that orientates – generating the growth of continuous learners and unlearners through your understanding and management of change.
4. Leadership that focuses – sustaining the direction of solution architects through your problem-solving and decision-making.
5. Leadership that aligns – connecting the vision, intention and impact of responsible citizens through your values-based leadership styles.
6. Leadership that enriches – cultivating team creators through the location of your purpose in your practice for the sake of people, place and planet.

Before we do this, however, we would like to dig deeper into the purpose and practice of game changers. Our global research program conducted through CIRCLE over the past decade has taught us much about the importance of leaders developing a sense of purpose grounded in an appreciation of people, place and planet. Catherine Misson, principal emeritus at Havergal College in Toronto, Canada, and former principal at Melbourne Girls' Grammar, explains this first aspect well. She emphasises how, as game changers, we must recognise that we must also cultivate a deep and sincere empathy for the human condition and how it might flourish.

## GAME CHANGER INSIGHT

*'I really do believe the research that those who will thrive in this fourth industrial revolution era in the fully digitalised economy are going to be the humans who can relate in powerful and positive ways, and are incredibly articulate, and can take others with them in the direction of what is best for them and for others.'*

**Catherine Misson**

Helping young people to grow and make progress in this way comes about during a natural and normal model of inside-out development that we call *The Pathway to Excellence*. This model sees learners embark on a personal journey of exploration, encounter and discovery as they:

1. learn the self-awareness of knowing themselves through asking, 'Who am I?'
2. live in relationships built by earning their place through asking, 'Where do I fit in?'
3. lead as a servant who goes on a journey from 'me' to 'you' to 'us' through asking, 'How can I best serve others?'
4. work vocationally and find their calling by asking, 'Whose am I?'

As game changers, we use the same developmental process. We use the process to grow in our competencies while we model, coach and scaffold the adaptive expertise, emotional competency and self-efficacy that we strive to pass on to our students, teachers, leaders and school teams so that they might flourish. We:

1. learn – influencing through the development of education as a research-driven instructional leader
2. live – inspiring through the development of culture as a growth-minded change leader
3. lead – directing through the development of strategy and leadership as a mission-oriented servant leader
4. work – motivating through the development of systems and structures as an evidence-based high-performance leader.

Our leadership as game changers, therefore, needs to influence, inspire, direct and motivate others to create today's learning for tomorrow's world. It should begin with who we are as people, flow into who we want to become and be demonstrated through our actions in service of others. Our service as game changers needs to be grounded in deliberate and targeted action as we learn, live, lead and work. It needs to align vision with intention and means to achieve better outcomes for more learners.

The following sections of this chapter explore each of these competencies. You will have an opportunity to reflect on your strengths and potential areas for development at the end of each section. We conclude the chapter by reflecting how these four competencies can be aligned with the graduate outcomes of a school for tomorrow and integrated into the capabilities of leadership in action. This, in turn, lays the foundation for the rest of this book.

## LEARN

To lead the way we learn in a school for tomorrow we need to influence through the development of education as a research-driven instructional leader. This means we need to support the creation and flourishing of a research-driven community of inquiry and practice that educates students to learn the character, competency and wellness required to flourish in their world.

The community of inquiry and practice in a school needs to be founded on the premise that all might find a deep sense of belonging and earn their place within it. For this to occur, that community needs to cultivate a growth mindset, empower learners and personalise learning so that all can learn self-awareness through asking the question 'Who am I?' as the first step on The Pathway to Excellence. The rush to agency without first understanding and getting the scope and sequence right can trip up any well-intentioned educational resolve. As Nikki Kirkup, principal of The Knox School, Victoria, makes clear, we need to understand that if we don't build the culture, protocols and systems that allow learners to operate in a holistic fashion – noting particularly the interdependence of wellbeing and academic growth – we will end up warping how the whole ecosystem works.

> **GAME CHANGER INSIGHT**
>
> *'Good learning is holistic. It always has to be. It has to be a match between the wellbeing and the academic. And it's not a binary view. It's not either/or. We have to be really careful that we're thinking holistically as learners ourselves.'*
>
> **Nikki Kirkup**

Game changers who influence as research-driven instructional leaders understand the primacy of an education for character, competency and wellness in a school for tomorrow. They recognise that through a blend of explicit and implicit, deliberate and spontaneous character learning (as illustrated in figure 1.1), schools must seek, above all, to grow the character of the whole person. This will be expressed in and guided by the graduate outcomes we referred to in the prologue (see page 4). These indicate what sort of person the community wants to foster and how we understand what it means for them to be ready to thrive in their world. If we are to influence the development of a research-driven community of inquiry and practice in a school in this fashion, then we need to understand who we are as a school, what the purpose of our shared endeavour might be and what this might look like in practice.

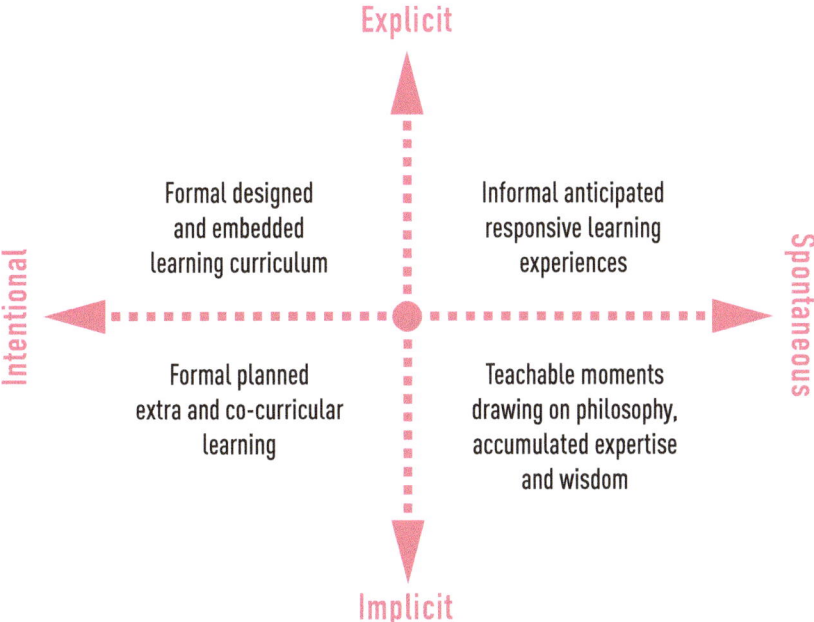

Figure 1.1: Character learning in a school for tomorrow

*The Way* is a term that we at a School for tomorrow. use to describe a research-driven and evidence-based approach to building a human-centred, technologically enriched, people, place and planet conscious, and intentionally purposeful ecosystem for schooling that responds to the new social contract for education: today's learning for tomorrow's world. The Way provides educators with an approach to building the education, culture, leadership and performance that equips, empowers and enables students to develop character, competencies and wellness on The Pathway to Excellence.

## Understanding The Way

Let's now focus on eight fundamental learnings that we have derived from our global research to help game changers understand The Way and how it operates in a future-fit learning community to promote student learning on The Pathway to Excellence.

1. Aspiration: we are called as educators to help others to strive for excellence and to develop their character, competency and wellness.

It starts with aspiration. What makes an education excellent is the quality and consistency of the education for character, competency and wellness that underpins it. In other words, when the character of an education is defined by, framed within and aligned with a community's aspirations for its graduates, then we begin to see what an education can really do. It's more than just a series of learning activities pursued for their own sake. Our research shows that the fundamental purpose of an excellent education should be the development of the whole character of the learner.

2. Purpose: character is why we do school.

We move next to think through the purpose of what we do at school in helping students to form the character they need to flourish in their world. The development of whole young people of character begins with how they wrestle with their own sense of who they should be (realisation) and what people expect of them (replication). As they do this, they begin to work out how they might belong more fully to their communities, fulfil their possibility and live with the integrity of a set of beliefs about what is good and right. This is the most fundamental reason for any school to exist. We believe that this process of wrestling with and developing character is at the heart of the purpose of any school.

3. Teacher voice and agency: we teach who we are and what we believe is important.

Teachers are the most important agents for supporting the character development of their students. What teachers think and feel about character and its relationship to their educational purpose both shapes and directs the development, attainment and measurement of civic, performance and moral character, the expression of these in their related qualities and competencies, and the demonstration of their attainment in a set of desired graduate outcomes in a school.

4. Shared model: character is the whole work of a school.

As part of our community of inquiry and practice, we need to build a shared understanding of our character work individually and collectively. How we think about the reason for our practice in building student character and connect this to the context, design and experiences of character learning across all aspects of a school can help us to locate and assess our work through a coherent and collaborative model of character education. This model, when shared among the members of the community, can be used to describe why, how and what learning occurs within our community of inquiry and practice towards the attainment of our desired graduate outcomes.

5. Apprenticeship and community: character development relies on designed learning relationships.

The impact of character learning in a school is largely the product of both specific and broader learning relationships that are designed to promote growth in character, competency and wellness. As mentioned earlier, character apprenticeships are the primary pedagogy of a school. As illustrated in figure 1.2, we see character apprenticeship as a progression from *articulates* to *reflects* to *explores* as a novice, then from *models* to *coaches* to *scaffolds* as an expert. Through these specific designed relationships, learners begin as novices; acquire adaptive expertise and self-efficacy from their chosen mentors, teachers and coaches; grow in voice, agency and advocacy over time; and eventually take on their own novices to pass on what they have learned in turn. All learners should also be brought together and equipped, empowered and enabled by a community of inquiry and practice whose work should be sharply focused on improving attainment of their school's graduate outcomes.

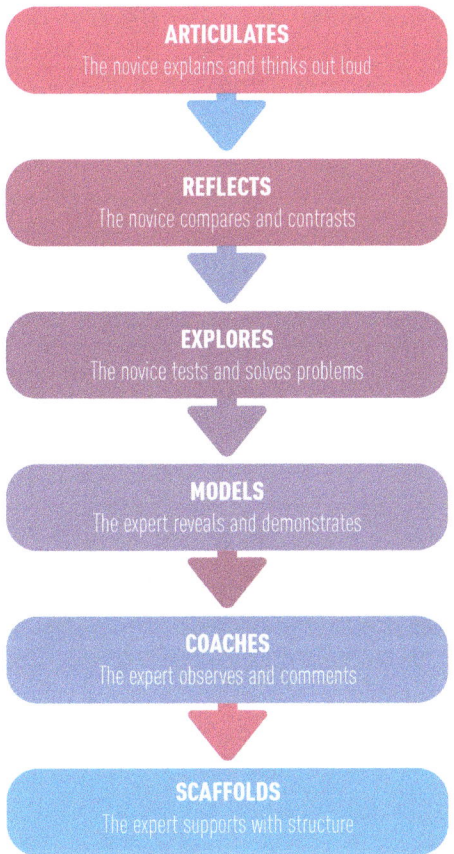

Figure 1.2: Character apprenticeship

6. Strategy: an education for character, competency and wellness works best when it's deliberate, targeted and intentional.

The quality and consistency of the attainment of a school's graduate outcomes by its learners reflect that school's willingness to embrace the need for strategic educational development that embeds character, competency and wellness into every facet of school life in a deliberate, targeted and intentional way. This requires the adoption of a strategic approach to building the right learning culture. It also requires collaborative development of a conceptual and documentary framework for education that will help the school move beyond just being intentional to becoming a school for tomorrow in every respect.

7. Character leadership: school leaders know the way, go the way and show the way forward.

School leaders build character capital in a learning community through their character labour, especially through their own role-modelling and by demonstrating positive leadership in action in accordance with The Way to develop the character, competency and wellness of their students, teachers and school teams. Their educational efficacy results from their will and their capacity to embed a shared commitment to 'what we want, why we want it and how we do it' in articulating, reflecting and exploring the embedding of shared purpose in practice. To this end, the leaders of our educational institutions need to be game changers who make real change in the culture, systems and structures of their learning communities to realise an education for character, competency and wellness.

8. Achievement: a good school focuses on getting the fundamentals of the education of the whole person right, but a great school assembles the ingredients of high-performance learning culture in delivering this education to achieve its graduate outcomes.

Our research has identified a 'secret sauce' with which great schools equip, empower and enable their learners. The ingredients begin with aspiration, a sense of kinship and pathways to success. Great schools blend these ingredients according to taste and apply this sauce liberally throughout all of their strategy and operations to inspire, challenge and support learners to grow in the character, competency and wellness they need to achieve their graduate outcomes and thrive in their world. This high-performance culture fosters a sense of belonging to and engagement in school, the fulfilment of potential through the pursuit of excellence by young people with adaptive expertise and self-efficacy, and the doing of what is good and right according to the ethos of the school community. As a consequence, it keeps learners in their groove through their practice and holds them to their educational purpose.

So what does this mean for us? How might we take these learnings and apply them to our leadership practice? As research-driven instructional leaders who are seeking to influence the growth of others, we need to be committed to growing and improving through our lives and be prepared for a lifetime of continuous learning and unlearning ourselves. This is why the most critical leadership capability to help us influence as research-driven instructional leaders is orientating through understanding and managing change.

Our leadership purpose as game changers should be to meet the challenges of preparing students to thrive in their world by building a future-fit learning community. A future-fit learning community steps forward and up together into a preferred future where vision and vocabulary are shared, values and value propositions are agreed by the school community, and the velocity, shape and trajectory of change are designed and implemented to meet the needs of internal and external contexts.

All student learning journeys are formed through the individual attainment of adaptive expertise and self-efficacy within the collective culture of a school. These journeys are enhanced by a shared commitment to continuous learning. *Continuous learning* is a flexible online and offline approach to the design, development and delivery of learning and teaching that allows all to access learning from their own location – anytime, anywhere, by anyone. Continuous learning does not prescribe a particular pedagogical approach. Rather, it supports transformation of the learner through a combination of teacher-directed, student-centred and student-led approaches in the curriculum and co-curriculum. This takes place within an evidence-based and research-driven community of inquiry and practice that is purposeful in supporting students to:

- grow in their voice, agency and advocacy through increasing self-determination in their learning
- make progress in developing their character, competency and wellness through relationships of character apprenticeship within the whole work of the school
- achieve success through the attainment of mastery of the graduate outcomes required to thrive in tomorrow's world.

> ## (!!) ENCOUNTER AND RESPOND
>
> We invite you to encounter the following extract from a School for tomorrow.'s research archive and respond to the reflective question at the end of the passage:
>
> *If we as game changers in a School for tomorrow. are going to exercise the competency to learn to build the future-fit culture of growth-minded change needed to design and deliver an education for character, competency and wellness, then we need to understand that the starting point for our leadership is understanding that the hearts of our students, teachers, leaders and school teams must be with us. Our leadership work with them cannot start in the cognitive domain; we need to work first in the affective domain to help people to grow, become change-ready, transform themselves and transform the school itself. It's always hearts before heads when we lead learning.*
>
> How might you learn to influence the development of education as a research-driven instructional leader by placing hearts before heads?

## LIVE

To lead how we live in a school for tomorrow we need to inspire through the development of culture as a growth-minded change leader. We need to cultivate within our community of inquiry and practise a disposition for change, align decisions and standards, and share in a language for learning that contributes to the progress and wellness of all. Why do we need to default towards change-mindedness rather than preserving the status quo? Greg Miller, former principal of St Luke's Catholic College and current principal of Chevalier College, puts forward a compelling case.

> **GAME CHANGER INSIGHT**
>
> *'We know that the world is changing. Those changes began twelve, ten years ago with iPhones, and portability and mobility of information at anywhere, any time. And we've been talking about it, well, for over a decade now. But the model hasn't changed yet. Yet, the world has changed in leaps and bounds. And the old industrial model of having chairs and desks in rows for students to sit at and look to the front to be the one font of information, that teacher. It's just busted. It's broken.'*
>
> Greg Miller

If the model for education is broken, then we must transform it and ourselves to meet the needs of our changing world. As game changers, we need to recognise that the members of a school community that takes this work of transformation seriously must co-create an agreed rationale, a shared approach to change readiness and a clear map for organisational development throughout their community. This needs to enable all to grow to become the people they need to be and to live well in relationships built by earning their places through asking the question 'Where do I fit in?' – the second step on The Pathway to Excellence.

Game changers who inspire transformation through growth-minded change culture understand the impact that a disposition towards learning has on how the members of a community relate to each other, work together and achieve success in their mission to prepare graduates with the character, competency and wellness to thrive in their world. A disposition for learning in a school for tomorrow is about the willingness to encourage a trajectory from progress to change to transformation for learners within an educational organisation.

It's also about the underlying growth of all contributors to the community of inquiry and the practice that allows this. As mentioned earlier, we need to help all learners find a voice with which they can contribute positively and meaningfully among and through these relationships over the course of a lifetime. To this voice must be added agency and advocacy, so that learners can put the ideas they voice into action, then test and refine them to determine their impact on and for others.

We need to help learners to expand their understanding of voice, agency and advocacy by acknowledging and taking responsibility for their interactions with others and the impact that this has. They should seek answers to fundamental questions about self-awareness, relationship, service and vocation as they transition from the early years of life in their families to seeking their own places in the world. Little children learn about becoming good people from their family; bigger children and adolescents learn about this from their friends, peers and teachers. All learners engage in their own intentional and reflective communities of inquiry and practice, which are most typically focused on the relationality and close friendships that are appropriate to their age and stage.

We know that while learners want to have fun with their friends, they are also motivated to learn from and with them; they rely on each other to bear witness to, to practice and to try out what it means to be a good person. They grow in character through their engagement in the whole life of their school and the community in which this is based.

In other words, the context of values, beliefs, history and traditions really matters in leading culture. We derive this context most significantly from our community. We need to understand where and who we have come from if we are to move forward with success. This does not mean we remain in the past and default to the status quo. We can pay respect to what was, keep what remains relevant and develop new solutions to help us to chart our way with progress. We can also develop the openness that acknowledges the new and the different for the potential that they have to add to the quality and richness of our lived experience. We can also develop the humility and gratitude that comes from understanding that nothing comes to us by entitlement or as a matter of course. In becoming adults, we have to earn our place.

The present and future complexities of our world call on all of us to take action individually and collectively in the long term to arrest the alarming trends that science warns and politicians argue about. There is much that we must prepare for on a global scale while also attending to the everyday matters of life: relationships, family, education, jobs, housing and so on. There are both practical and philosophical implications for how we learn within and from community and why we make the choices we do about how best to prepare ourselves to live and be well.

Wellness is how we experience and feel about health and happiness in the world. Our wellness is influenced by our health (physical, psychological, emotional and spiritual), our satisfaction with the lives we are leading and the sense of purpose and connectedness we have. Character is directly affected by wellness; how well we are is so very important to how we live our lives and who we are becoming through all of our social relationships and educational experiences on our pathways to excellence.

The personal journeys of our students as they grow in the character, competency and wellness they need to flourish, therefore, need to connect the development of their voice, agency, advocacy and wellness to the essential questions that they all have about who they are and who they are becoming. Their journeys need to support them to find answers to these questions. The power of this process of inquiry to help all learners live better lives, to help them feel they are making a difference in the world and to help them to know that they are getting somewhere must be embedded in how we talk about it. It must be so significant, so rich and perhaps even so disruptive of their frames of mind that it compels them to sit up and take notice. It must force them to want to do something about it. It must make them commit to a journey of learning towards character, to explore, discover and encounter experience, progress and success on The Pathway to Excellence. Students realise that it's not about any one person – me or you. It's about us and how we live together well.

Our leadership purpose as game changers in this context must be centred on building a healthy school culture. Our focus in this respect must be on the fundamental purpose of the school: designing and delivering an education for character, competency and wellness. Being capable of focusing through problem-solving and decision-making and also enriching through cultivating our teams helps us to inspire as growth-minded change leaders who seek to recognise and enhance the common humanity of all involved in the enterprise of a school.

We would argue that promoting holistic, growth-minded change culture and the organisational maturity of a school is essential to the long-term sustainability and achievement of the shared purpose of an education for character, competency and wellness. From our research we believe there to be six aspects of a school for tomorrow that we should develop an intimate knowledge of to influence growth that will inspire people to nurture the culture that we want: promoting school character, climate and culture; leadership of the educational program; teacher effectiveness in growing the whole person; student educational experiences and outcomes; strategic and operational alignment; and teacher professionalism in a community of inquiry and practice.

So much of this comes down to the doing of the culture work of modelling, scaffolding and coaching people in articulating, reflecting on and exploring the disposition towards change through our relationships of character apprenticeship. In schools, or any organisation for that matter, achieving change is really about supporting successful adult learning. As we have noted, if adults are going to learn we must start by connecting with the heart before we try to convince the head. We need to allow people time to do this and to grow in this way in a non-threatening fashion.

> ## (II) ENCOUNTER AND RESPOND
>
> We invite you to encounter the following extract from a School for tomorrow.'s research archive and respond to the reflective question at the end of the passage:
>
> *The growth-minded change culture of a school for tomorrow can be traced back to how we lead a community towards a shared disposition to ask questions that challenge the status quo, develop answers that reveal a shared language of learning and the capacity to define a strategy that is singularly focused on improving outcomes for more learners who have the adaptive expertise and self-efficacy to thrive in their world. It requires all to be inspired by the discoveries and process of continuous learning and unlearning. They need to want to do this together as servants of a community who relate well to each other in pursuit of their shared goal of the transformation of themselves, of each other and of the community as a whole. That's the true work of the leader who inspires growth-minded change.*
>
> How might you learn to inspire others through the development of culture as a growth-minded change leader by modelling the disposition to ask questions that challenge the status quo?

# LEAD

To lead the way all of us lead in a school for tomorrow we need to direct by developing strategy and leadership as a mission-oriented servant leader. As we help to build better outcomes for all learners in partnership with schools and other educational organisations through our work with a School for tomorrow., we often take stock to ask ourselves, our students and our families about what really makes a difference in describing the narrative arc of a school's culture yesterday, today and tomorrow. So often the answer that we see lies in the quality of the leadership in a school. It is leadership at all levels that helps students and teachers to connect with each other meaningfully and purposefully. It is leadership that helps people to prioritise unlocking the potential of learners to meet and exceed expectations above all other tasks. And such leadership needs to model and scaffold for our learners the entrepreneurial mindset identified by Jan Owen AM, co-convenor of Learning Creates Australia.

> ## GAME CHANGER INSIGHT
>
> 'If there was ever a time when there's going to be a need for an entrepreneurial mindset – and I don't mean a world of zillions of many entrepreneurs, but I mean an entrepreneurial mindset and worldview or way of thinking – this is going to be the time.'
>
> Jan Owen AM

It is leadership characterised by a curious and adventurous approach that unlocks the door to the possibility of becoming a school for tomorrow. This type of leadership requires courage and compassion. It is about becoming a true servant who goes on a journey from 'me' to 'you' to 'us' through asking the question 'How can I best serve others?' – the third question on The Pathway to Excellence. As we have noted in this chapter, it is also about building character capital in a learning community through character labour and using this to turn vision into intention and then means through high-performance learning culture.

To lead like this requires us to show the way forward for others. We need to help them to reimagine education and what it might and should become: today's learning for tomorrow's world. Game changers who build cultures of excellence in leadership and learning in their schools direct as mission-oriented servants. They cultivate communities of inquiry and practice that are dedicated to the attainment of the character, competency and wellness that their graduates need to thrive in their world. Leading for this begins with asking and answering the questions that will help a school make the right choices about its future. It moves onto creating a strategy that will facilitate the realisation of the purpose and mission of the school, and then finally to developing a shared vision for how strategic learning capacity might be increased to these ends.

The leadership capabilities that help us to direct as mission-oriented servant leaders are informing through creating and communicating vision and aligning through values-based leadership styles. Leading through strategic intent draws a school together by building trust and leading through narrative creates shared purpose in a school. This is characterised by the way leaders promote openness and responsibility, establish commitment to a common aspiration and resource for long-term success.

As leaders, we therefore need to aim to be the very best we can be at leading and learning within an evidence-based and research-driven discourse that is built on asking and answering questions about what might be done better towards this purpose. We need to be prepared to make good decisions about and on behalf of our students, their families and the community when this time comes. There are typically five lenses through which a school for tomorrow strategises what to do and how to do it:

1. Future focused

Are decisions emerging from an inclination to move forward to meet the needs of the future?

2. Character rich

Are decision-makers considering the ways in which any and all decisions both model and promote the desired character, competency and wellness for students and other members of the school community?

3. Action oriented

Are stakeholders committed to both taking the initiative to act and ensuring concrete actions to improving outcomes (especially student outcomes)?

4. Inclusive and empowering

Do decision-makers make decisions in the best interests of the voice, agency and wellbeing of every and each stakeholder in terms of diversity, equity and inclusion – particularly the students?

5. Reflective inquiry

Do decision-makers habitually ask searching and meaningful questions while moving through well-rehearsed and considered multistage processes that ask them to contemplate context, balance the best of external research with internal evidence of impact, generate a range of options and select the best available course of action to achieve the task at hand?

A further key element of strategic leadership for the culture of a school for tomorrow concerns generating the disposition towards testing the quality of its decisions and warranting the integrity of its practice, particularly in the light of the research about how communities of inquiry and practice operate in great schools.

We believe schools and their teachers should warrant their practice according to these five characteristics or approaches. This means that they take responsibility for demonstrating what they have learned, how they have learned it and assessing the progress they have made towards their goals. This should include validating the quality and consistency of the delivery of graduate outcomes based on character, competency and wellness, as well as the essential processes by which a school might attain them. Essential to this is evaluating the depth of investigation into the idea of character, the immersion of character leadership in every part of the school, the richness of character apprenticeship as the key pedagogy for the learning experience, the shared discipline in delivering excellence in learning experience and outcomes, the success in cultivating emerging student voice and agency, and the rigour of teacher professionalism. How teachers and leaders build a case for and warrant their practice provides the critical accountability for ensuring the continuing presence and evolving nature of growth-minded change culture in a school for tomorrow that is focused on building the adaptive expertise, emotional competency and self-efficacy of learners who are equipped to thrive in their world.

Building the strategic learning capacity to do this involves establishing and enhancing a culture of aspiration and performance within the community. This begins with how we model hope, gratitude and a focus on the future. The community (and everyone in it) needs to set high expectations and provide correspondingly high support; the assumption that this is being done is too frequently revealed to be inconsistent with the reality within schools of all types. The expectation for student growth and achievement should be based on the belief that all children are capable of success; children should be supported to set goals and achieve them regardless of their background and socioeconomic situation. Schools must have clear and ambitious support for students and teachers – ideally involving students and teachers in setting those standards – and systems of clear communication, reflection, review and feedback on achievement. At the same time, they need to pay attention to what works and what doesn't work in making these standards realisable. In defining and pursuing a vision, schools should attend to leading in practice (drawing on evidence and exemplars of successful education, both locally and internationally), pay close attention to measuring success and feedback loops, and understand the state and needs of the systems that support learning and innovation.

> ## ⏸ ENCOUNTER AND RESPOND
>
> We invite you to encounter the following extract from a School for tomorrow.'s research archive and respond to the reflective question at the end of the passage:
>
> *As mission-oriented servant leaders, we need to be purposeful about creating a strategy for the future of the school and its community. We should align the operations of all aspects of daily life in the community to their intent. We should be inherently dissatisfied with the status quo and be prepared to redesign the vision, direction, structures and processes required to create a school for tomorrow. We need to apply models and frameworks of positive and authentic leadership that balance the need to honour the past and address the demands of the present while prioritising looking forward to a preferred future. We need to be both responsible citizens who are prepared to put the common interest and the needs of others before ourselves, as well as leaders for the future who translate a vision of this into a shared story of progress.*
>
> How can you as a game changer learn to direct the strategy and leadership of a school and its community towards the achievement?

## WORK

As we lead the way we work in a school for tomorrow we motivate through the development of systems and structures as an evidence-based high-performance leader. Each member of the community has a responsibility in time to motivate one other to become evidence-based champions of high-performance learning culture through our work within the systems and structures that improve outcomes for all learners. Dr Deborah Netolicky, head of teaching and learning at St Mark's Anglican Community School, Western Australia, reminds us that, as leaders who help others move towards this goal of high performance, we need to balance high support and high challenge.

## GAME CHANGER INSIGHT

*'The learning that's most likely to be transformational has a balance of high support and high challenge. So there's high care, but there's also kind of a high level of challenge and I guess something to get our heads around. It's targeted. It's ongoing. It's differentiated. There's a sense of voice and choice for the educator. And, within a school environment, it's really linked to doing the right thing for our context and knowing our people.'*

*Dr Deborah Netolicky*

As game changers who lead the working culture of our communities, we need to understand that what we create as a standard is really an expression of the aspiration for (not necessarily the experience of) every community member. Such standards should always be personalised to the individual, aligned to community expectations for a collective experience and integrated within every aspect of a school's daily life. When doing this we need support and challenge all in the learning community to commit to their calling, bring together the compelling narrative, describe and measure our performance, and define the narrative and role of the community of inquiry and practice that will help everyone to work vocationally and find their calling. This is understood most clearly in asking, 'Whose am I?' – the fourth and final question of the inside-out developmental process of The Pathway to Excellence.

Game changers who motivate as evidence-based leaders of high-performance learning in the work culture of a school for tomorrow motivate people to develop their organisational, professional and personal competencies and to align their performance with their school's social contract to prepare young people to thrive in their world. But what is high-performance learning in the work culture of a school? What do families want for the education of their children? How well are schools fulfilling the expectations of society about the purpose of education? Having learned over the past decade from the a School for tomorrow. global network of schools, we can share what people have told us about how they want high-performance learning to look in the work culture of their schools.

The first thing to note is that the expectations of stakeholders are overwhelmingly expressed in terms of the growth of the whole person and the development of the character, competencies and wellness that comprise this through providing a whole education. Very few specifically point to one field of achievement as the desirable goal. High approval is given to schools that routinely meet and exceed these stakeholder expectations for a strong experience of a whole education. In other words, when stakeholders believe that schools do a good job in educating their students, they like what they experience and are supportive of their schools. We are also beginning to develop a clearer understanding of what an industry standard of high-performance learning culture might look like, how schools can move towards it if they are still developing their practice and how they can achieve it by developing this culture in a future-ready and future-fit school.

A future-ready and future-fit school demonstrates a shared vision and vocabulary for its preferred future, an agreed value proposition for what it delivers and a commitment to change, the velocity, shape and trajectory of which have all been designed and implemented to attend to the demands and pressures of the school's external and internal contexts. It delivers an excellent education for character that is founded on fit-for-purpose graduate outcomes, their key qualities and capabilities (character, communication, change readiness, creative and critical thinking, citizenship, and collaboration), and the expression of these in a curriculum that shapes its educational philosophies, programs and activities towards a preferred future. A future-fit school should therefore become an evidence-based community of inquiry and practice that is focused on improving outcomes for more learners by:

- providing a whole education (emphasising the deliberate, targeted and intentional centrality of character, competency and wellness in an excellent education)
- meeting expectations for a whole education (cooking up the secret sauce of high-performance culture in driving the character of an excellent school)
- achieving standards for whole education (by balancing purpose, growth and relationship in the character of a leader and the leader of character in excellent schools).

Integral to any evaluation of the leadership of high-performance culture within a school will be conscientious attendance to the factor that research tells us makes the greatest difference to the quality and consistency of student learning outcomes: staff professional learning. Understanding the learning journeys of individual teachers and other members of a school community requires a respect for the difficulties that confront individuals during this process of acquiring and maintaining a level of conscious competence characterised by self-efficacy and adaptive expertise. In this context especially, the leadership capability that most helps us to motivate as evidence-based high-performance leaders is strengthening through disciplined and purpose-driven practice.

This requires us to have in mind a clear picture of what the end product of our labour in the professional learning of our colleagues might be. It is clear that the leadership of learning work must do more than facilitate the 'doing' of professional learning and the promotion of collaboration among our colleagues to gather an evidence basis for what we do. It needs to have a shared and deeply ingrained commitment to doing those things that will generate the learning needed by a community of inquiry and practice to produce improved outcomes for all learners.

## (II) ENCOUNTER AND RESPOND

We invite you to encounter the following extract from a School for tomorrow.'s research archive and respond to the reflective question at the end of the passage:

*An ecosystem that is home to continuous high-performance learning and improvement requires a school for tomorrow to become a home for the continual transformation of the workforce talent. Game changers need to recognise that, like adolescence, adulthood must be a time for ongoing growth and development. As with all character development, it starts with belonging, the attainment of possibility and the doing of what is good and right. Adults will do this work if they connect to it effectively and can justify it cognitively. In other words, we need to start with the heart before we move to the head. We need to help people to build adaptive expertise, emotional competency and self-efficacy in their roles within relationships of character apprenticeship that take years (not weeks) to mature – and also know that these relationships will ebb and flow in different ways and at different paces. We need to create the conditions of psychological safety under which all learners can take the risks necessary for exploration of new modes of mindset, thinking and behaviour that might create a trajectory for transformation that interweaves all of these things simultaneously.*

How might you champion the conditions of psychological safety to build a culture of high-performance learning that, in turn, grows other game changers?

## LEADERSHIP IN ACTION AS A GAME CHANGER

So, your leadership as a game changer starts with your inside-out development as you learn, live, lead and work with your people so they might thrive in our world. You will therefore also need to know how to capture the energy and imagination of people at an organisational level. You will need to learn how to use real emotional competency to lead and move the organisation forward by helping people to acquire the mastery, autonomy and purpose to grow, make progress and succeed. As Canadian theorist, researcher, prolific author in education and *Game Changers* guest Michael Fullan (2011) would argue, if you focus mostly on the work of individuals and the use of technology for its own sake, and do all of this in a piecemeal fashion, you won't get far. You need to be systematic about an approach to leadership in action that focuses on improved outcomes for all learners by building capacity, teamwork and shared practice.

What we have found from our research is that effective game changers understand how to articulate and enact concrete and positive capabilities of this leadership in action to learn, live, lead and work in a way that speaks to our times. What might this leadership in action as a game changer look like?

Let's think about the outcomes we want our learners to achieve and how we might align our leadership to them. In the prologue and earlier in this chapter we mentioned a range of graduate outcomes that we can use to guide the learning ecosystem of a school for tomorrow to help learners to thrive in our world. Thriving in the context of these graduate outcomes means human beings applying their character, competency and wellness to experience success in a world that wants and needs them to:

- have the integrity to lead meaningful lives as good people
- manage complexity with authenticity as future builders
- grow and transform themselves as continuous learners and unlearners
- provide sustainable direction to the world as solution architects
- balance the local, the regional and the global with perspective as responsible citizens
- work well in relationship with others to bring success and fulfilment for all as team creators.

If we want to change the game of school so that we are truly helping our learners to thrive in this way, then we need to form and align our character and competencies to these graduate outcomes. After all, if we don't model, coach and scaffold these values, intentions and actions, then how can we expect our students to grow in the same fashion themselves?

Ultimately, our global research program has taught us that growing into and exercising the character of game changers in future-fit schools is a process that can be understood and reflected on through the six key capabilities of leadership in action. These six capabilities align with the graduate outcomes for learners in the following way:

1. Leadership that strengthens

Do I bring the values and value of good people through disciplined and purpose-driven practice?

2. Leadership that informs

Do I share the compelling narrative of future builders by creating and communicating vision?

3. Leadership that orientates

Do I generate the growth of continuous learners and unlearners by understanding and managing change?

4. Leadership that focuses_

Do I sustain the direction of solution architects by solving problems and making decisions?

5. Leadership that aligns

Do I connect the vision, intention and impact of responsible citizens through values-based leadership styles?

6. Leadership that enriches

Do I cultivate team creators by locating purpose, people, place and practice?

It is these capabilities of leadership in action to which we will turn our attention in the next six chapters of this book. Each will be explored through the integrated and sequential inside-out development process that characterises how we learn, live, lead and work on a personal journey of exploration, encounter and discovery.

# CHAPTER 2
## Leadership that strengthens

**VALUES AND VALUE LADEN: INTRODUCING LEADERSHIP THAT STRENGTHENS**

To help a school on its quest to honour the new social contract of education and support its students to thrive in their world, we will need the strength to step forward together into a preferred future. In this future, the vision and the vocabulary for education are shared; the velocity, the shape and the trajectory of change are designed and implemented to meet internal and external needs; and the values and value propositions of the school are agreed on by the school community. Throughout the school network, we will need to model and support relationships that demonstrate integrity, meaningfulness and the exchange of both of these values and value propositions over time.

As leaders in schools, therefore, we need to strengthen people, we need to strengthen institutions and we need to strengthen the societies they serve. We do this first through the character work of embedding agreed values in all that a community does and experiences. We also do this by bringing our learners and their families the value or benefit of improved outcomes that flow from these values. This is what we mean by a values and value proposition: building the civic, performance and moral character of a community character in both abstract and tangible ways.

What might be the object of this confluence of values and value proposition for a future-ready and future-fit school? Stephanie McConnell, founding principal of the Lindfield Learning Village, New South Wales, emphasises that, above all else, our service as school leaders needs to have a clear aim.

> **GAME CHANGER INSIGHT**
>
> 'My belief is that the purpose of schooling is to equip young people with the mindset that they need to thrive in the world beyond school.'
>
> Stephanie McConnell

CIRCLE's work suggests that this mindset involves fluency in the adaptive expertise and self-efficacy students need for success in a world that expects more of them than of any previous generation. Many schools around the world agree with this thinking and are currently investigating ways to bring the values and value of this to their learners. But what a learning community believes it values is one thing; how consistently and how well it acts in accordance with these values to bring values and value to its members is another – and that depends on the quality and consistency of our character as leaders who strengthen. This is, ultimately, the test of the leadership capability of disciplined and purpose-driven practice. High-quality leadership strengthens a school community by bringing it together to agree to and then enact a values and value proposition – such as that proposed by McConnell – for its members individually, in groups and as a whole.

So, our schools are made stronger when we use disciplined and purpose-driven practice to bring the values present in the character of good people to life in the experiences of the members of our communities of inquiry and practice – and through the character capital this generates in these same communities. They are also strengthened when we work to make explicit and tangible the often-implicit culture that is grounded in these moral values, while also generating the practical value of adaptive expertise, emotional competency and self-efficacy by cultivating accomplishment and achievement in the experiences of school members and graduates as they live, learn, lead and work.

In this chapter, we will look at leadership that strengthens through a School for tomorrow.'s four-step process of inside-out leadership development. In posing the question 'Who am I?' we will explore the character and purpose of strong leaders who improve the capacity of teams to build a culture that represents the values and value propositions of learning communities – particularly the graduate outcome of good people. We will examine the expectations for achievement-focused, disciplined and purpose-driven practice by asking, 'Where do I fit in?' In considering the question 'How can I best serve others?' we will reflect on the selflessness of leadership that strengthens and the key qualities of calmness, passion, optimism and perseverance. Finally, you will have the opportunity to respond to the question 'Whose am I?' by thinking through how you bring your own value to your school community with the leadership that strengthens.

## WHO AM I?

### Good people: The character of leaders who strengthen

What is character and what about it is so important to our leadership? What is a model of the character of a leader and the leader of character on which we might base the character of our own leadership?

Character is the way we live our lives; it's how we realise – through our actions – our values and beliefs about what is important to us. At a School for tomorrow. we have learned from conversations with hundreds of thousands of members of school communities around the world that character exists on three levels at the same time. As we strive to build the civic character that helps us gain a sense of belonging through our contributions to community, we also seek to demonstrate both performance character, through which we engage with possibility and fulfil our potential, and moral character, which informs what we believe is good and right. As we embark on a journey towards this character, we wrestle with both realising our own inner drive (our mark) and replicating the expectations of others (our measure). In this uncertain space, this wrestling with both leaving a mark and measuring up, that we reveal the strength of character that shows who we have been and who we are becoming.

When school leaders reveal this strength through their own character labour, we influence the character of a school and its people. By showing the way forward, we also encourage building the total amount of character labour (or 'character capital') shown by everyone within a school community. We do this especially through role-modelling. Our strength of character, therefore, requires leadership by example that is deeply connected to the core of the school's shared values and a willingness to undergo scrutiny of the effectiveness of this example.

The graduate outcome in a school for tomorrow most closely aligned to the leadership capability of strengthening is that of good people. Leaders who want to be game changers need to model through their own character what it means to be good people to the members of their communities, and then scaffold and coach these same competencies so that individuals grow in them and the community grows in character capital as a whole.

So, what do we mean by the term *good people*? When we spoke with school communities around the world about their expectations of the outcomes learners will demonstrate as they graduate from their schooling, they told us how they might learn, live, lead and work as good people.

**Learn**

Good people want to be people of good character, competence and wellness. Inspired by meaningfulness, they seek to demonstrate the mark and measure of a person of integrity who can navigate our world with civic behaviours characterised by respect, civility and consideration for others; performance comprising purpose, persistence and reflection; and a moral code informed by courage, honesty and humility.

**Live**

They are committed to becoming virtuous people who have a coherent set of values and beliefs that guide them to do the right thing and to live a good life: their ethics. They use honesty, responsibility and courage to show the character required to stand strong in the face of adversity and place the needs of others before self-interest. They do their best to align their values, dispositions and actions (and the consequences of these actions).

**Lead**

They work towards improving their character. They recognise that building their character involves demonstrating integrity through aligning the values, dispositions and actions that are associated with civic character, performance character and moral character. This relies on demonstrating quality and consistency in the fulfilment of their obligations to others, reaching their potential and acting in accordance with their fundamental beliefs about what is good and right to do.

**Work**

They have a coherent set of values and beliefs that guide them to do the right thing. These are grounded in learning about character and helps them to understand how individuals and communities construct their sense of identity, values and ethics; acquire skills in encouraging character in themselves and others; maintain a disposition towards the self-discipline required for a purpose-driven and virtuous life; and build the capacity to reflect on the integrity of their character.

## Building culture: The purpose of leaders who strengthen

Modelling the values of their school and the character of good people is a strong starting point for our model of leadership, but game changers go further than this; they build the culture that spreads and strengthens the character of good people throughout their community. In this way, we can not only strengthen the character of the students, teachers and families of our school; we can also strengthen the character of the community itself.

As Nathan Chisholm, principal of Prahran High School, Victoria, makes clear to us, we need to do more than show the character of a leader. We also need to be leaders for character.

**GAME CHANGER INSIGHT**

*'One thing that to me I'm absolutely resolute on is that schools have a role to play in building character.'*

Nathan Chisholm

This includes how we set about designing and implementing the substance and meaning of the educational program in a way that links a school's values to its value proposition. In this way, the efficacy of the leadership that strengthens a school's whole program results from the will and capacity of leaders. This occurs especially when they embed a shared commitment to the intention and practice of an education among the day to life of the community. It is this aggregation of habits, behaviours, rituals and artefacts that we call culture: what we want, why we want it and how we do it together in a community of inquiry and practice.

Our character leadership in practice can also be improved by linking it to a theory that explains the decisions that drive this intention and practice. We believe that an education for character and wellness is central to the mission for all schools that seek to respond to the new social contract of education:

preparing our graduates to thrive by designing and delivering today's learning for tomorrow's world.

We see in many schools that character leadership is envisaged more in the daily doing of the operational tasks within a highly situational and responsive practice than in the broader scope of a sense of purpose and a strategic intention. Perhaps this is a by-product of the busyness to which many school leaders might point if they had the time to comment!

Nonetheless, we believe that leaders in schools need to find the time to develop and reflect on a model of their leadership character that aligns values and intentions with concrete actions. Any model that they construct for their leadership will benefit from both clear alignment to the strategic educational intent of being a future-fit school and the operational soundness that can be found in implementing a plan for this specific intent.

So, we need to lead with the character of good people as game changers who embed this character within the shared values, intentions and actions of their school community. The character of the leader who strengthens needs to be directed towards building a future-fit school culture. School culture is the strategic lever that most influences an education for the character, competency and wellness that produces good people. Leaders who apply this character are focused on the fundamental purpose of a school of character: an education for character, competency and wellness. They earn a strong and credible reputation as a future-fit school. They focus on their organisational integrity by ensuring consistency in the application of their ethos, engagement with their community, thoroughness in their planning, the quality of their outcomes and the execution of their strategy. They also value the efficiency and efficacy of their processes across the domains of reputation, communication, evaluation, achievement, initiatives and relationships.

The key marker of success in such a school can be found in the resilience of its consensus about its ethos. The members of this sort of school community are true to the stated values and purpose of their school. They are strengthened by this ethos, particularly through the alignment of their stated – and unstated – culture. This is demonstrated in the connections between words and deeds in the community, within the daily activity of students, staff and leaders in particular. They agree on what matters to them. They encourage and reinforce this by promoting shared intentional, aspirational and practical values, intentions and principles that enable the community to withstand the challenges of conflicting goals and hidden assumptions about educational design and delivery.

All of this means that if we are going to build for ourselves the character of leaders who are game changers, we need to understand how our own current context is another stage in the learning journey of our schools and societies. This is because, in our times, the character of leadership in schools is inextricably bound up with helping communities to chart a way forward in a rapidly changing world. As game changers in education, we need to be those brave pioneers whose innovative ideas are shaping the landscape of schooling. We can't wait for permission. We need to be courageous enough through our leadership to make real change in our learning communities as we foster the growth of each young person in our care. We need to equip students with the necessary character, confidence and competencies to experience success on the pathways to excellence that will see them acquire the adaptive expertise and self-efficacy to flourish in a new world environment.

To build the right culture and to strengthen ourselves in the process, we need to sustain rich conversations with colleagues in education around the world about what is happening in education right now. We also need to continue learning about the capacity of our profession to effect significant changes in a constructive and effective manner. This is because what seemed impossible or undesirable in the recent past is now the new reality and we are all taking away from our immediate experience new understandings about providing an education that will equip students to thrive in this world. Our knowledge, skills, dispositions and learning habits are all changing – because they have to.

Leaders who strengthen need to imbue this work with courage and commitment. Tracey Breese, principal of the Hunter School of the Performing Arts and former principal of Kurri Kurri High School, both in New South Wales, comments on what this means to her in her typically direct and succinct fashion.

## GAME CHANGER INSIGHT

*'I think there's a moral imperative for us to continue to build amazing citizens of the future. And I don't believe the traditional system does that.'*

**Tracey Breese**

Leaders who strengthen by building culture, therefore, must be 'other-focused'. True service as leaders of communities means individuals and teams coming together and collaborating to model the character, create the model of learning and develop the culture of a school for tomorrow. There will be elements to this service that may be challenging. Many do not wish to hear or may only selectively hear what needs to happen to take the big step forward and up, or perhaps they may struggle to find the strength required to see it through. Yet the nature of this challenge to create a positive impact despite the obstacles presented along the way should not daunt us. The task of strengthening can and should be done.

>  **ENCOUNTER AND RESPOND**
>
> What defines your character and purpose as a leader who strengthens your school community?

## WHERE DO I FIT IN?

### The practice of a leader who strengthens

If it is the character of good people that underpins the character of the leader who strengthens and this character should be directed towards the work of building culture, then it will be the quality and consistency of how we exercise the leadership capability of disciplined and purpose-driven practice that will determine our success as game changers who strengthen.

Our work with school leaders in communities all around the world suggests a set of common leadership practices that are simultaneously disciplined and purposeful at both team and organisational levels in building culture. Tables 2.1 and 2.2 describe this practice.

## Table 2.1: Strengthening as a leader of a team

| | |
|---|---|
| **DISCIPLINED PRACTICE** | Gains mastery over physical and mental challenges and demonstrates satisfaction in response to imposed discipline, a sense of achievement and perseverance in the face of adversity. |
| | Shows consistent self-discipline by accepting the standards taught and applying them willingly and personally with increasing restraint and self-regulation. |
| | Influences and motivates team collective discipline through personal example, understanding of team members, creating positive and intentional culture, maintaining high standards, fair and ethical treatment of others, and effective communication. |
| **PURPOSE-DRIVEN PRACTICE** | Demonstrates an effective understanding of the key leadership tasks of setting direction and achieving the organisation's purpose, building the team, and growing the character, competency and wellness of its members. |
| | Employs a range of suitable and practical principles of leadership in action to create and sustain a culture that will help to fulfil the purpose of the school to provide today's learning for tomorrow's world. |
| | Demonstrates the character, competency and wellness to model the values, intentions and outcomes required to achieve the organisation's purpose. |

## Table 2.2: Strengthening as a leader of an organisation

| | |
|---|---|
| **DISCIPLINED PRACTICE** | Leads by example in the way they act, the way they spend their time and how they allocate resources according to organisational priorities based on purpose and culture. |
| | Demonstrates collaboration and cooperation without competing against other school leaders. |
| | Contributes effectively as a member of the broader school leadership team, community and network. |
| **PURPOSE-DRIVEN PRACTICE** | Focuses the work of teams on the vital work of the organisation. |
| | Brings strategic clarity to the priorities and work of teams. |
| | Reviews and aligns practice with the school's underlying philosophy, ethos and narrative for change rather than with past practice. |

# Disciplined and purposeful practice

What do we mean by disciplined and purpose-driven practice? Let's break this leadership functionality down into each component.

We see discipline as a state of mind that produces willing and intelligent support and appropriate conduct in pursuit of a purpose. It is usually acquired by teams in a three-stage process. At first, we model self-discipline as leaders and create the expectation that other team members will come to act with professional discipline. In time, as they meet the standards asked of them and receive positive feedback, team members will achieve the satisfaction of accomplishment that comes from disciplined behaviour and will build habits of restraint and self-regulation. Finally, team members will build a collective discipline that means they apply team standards and expectations voluntarily. They sacrifice their self-interest and ego in favour of the team's interests and the entire ecosystem, fostering an environment of mutual trust and confidence. In time, they will come to be the custodians and co-creators of these standards.

Throughout this three-stage process, role-modelling is (of course) essential. We have seen this already in how we learn, live, lead and work towards demonstrating the values, intentions and actions that comprise the culture of our school. We need to be the example that others follow, not the exception. The core of this insight is that we all have the same potential to be positive role models in the communities we lead. People are always watching what we say and do. When something is due, we need to be the first to complete it and to the highest standard. We need to give others something to aspire to, to do more than just the bare minimum for the sake of compliance.

Discipline also contributes to and is based on an effective learning environment. A continually improving, efficient and effective team relies on a high degree of discipline that ensures stability, promotes regular and psychologically safe patterns, and helps all members work toward realising their school's shared vision. We need to be voices, agents and advocates for the trust, confidence and mutual respect that will create this environment. What we do to ensure the fair, just and ethical treatment of members of our communities is crucial to maintaining high morale, as is how we instil a sense of purpose in what we do together.

We have noted that the essence of today's learning for tomorrow's world is about connecting our students to a life of purpose. All of us are learners. All of us need a sense of purpose, a compelling rationale for what it is that we do on our lifelong journey of exploration, encounter and discovery to answer the question 'Why?'

What is our purpose as game-changing leaders? If we are going to rise to the often heard but seldom understood challenge of twenty-first century education, what we do in schools must reflect a rationale that goes beyond the transmission of content. We must do what we can to support the transformation of people from who they are now to who they might become. Getting access to programs, completing courses of study and gaining qualifications are important vehicles for social mobility and practical preparation to learn, live, lead and work. However, there is more to thriving in our world than the ongoing exercise of these competencies and the technological innovations that might support them. Education must be more than drilling and skilling in the doing of things to prepare students for the next round of the doing of things. We need to make that difference that so many of us wanted to make when we went into education in the first place.

What is it, then, that will make the greatest difference in the lives of our students? What will help them create lives that are worthwhile and well-lived? We need to help the young people in our care to connect with something that goes beyond their own emotional, intellectual and physical selves. We need to show them that a journey of discovery in which they encounter self-awareness, relationship, service and vocation takes them beyond self-interest and towards selflessness. The key assumption that underpins this is that a life of giving to others is inherently transformative for our students. It has this impact because it gives them a genuine meaningfulness that can equip, empower and enable them with the character, competency and wellness they need to thrive, to lead a life of purpose.

From what we see in schools all around the world, we are convinced that every school needs to realise the possibility of a future with better outcomes for its learners. This must be cultivated in an ecosystem that is human centred; technologically enriched; people, place and planet conscious; and intentionally purposeful about designing and delivering a new social contract of education: today's learning for tomorrow's world.

So, what is the essence of today's learning for tomorrow's world? It's all about inspiring, challenging and supporting our students to connect with a life of purpose. We know that game changers around the world remain committed to creating learning communities that focus on the full flourishing of each young person in their care. Our passion is for helping students to discover what their purpose might be and how they might learn, live, lead and work in pursuit of it to become the best versions of themselves. This pathway to excellence is our purpose, our true calling, our vocation, our raison d'être as game changers.

When and how might leaders use discipline to strengthen the people, culture and institutions of a school community? How might leaders tie this act of strengthening to the achievement of those fundamental outcomes that honour the new social contract of education: today's learning for tomorrow's world?

Achievement is essential in any educational context. When, what and how learners achieve – when this achievement is articulated as expressions of character, competency and wellness in pursuit of agreed graduate outcomes – comprises the union of both the values and value proposition of a school. Therefore, when we work as leaders with our colleagues and the community more broadly to promote students' achievement in how they learn, live, lead and work, we are bringing tangible value to students' lives and to the lives of those around them.

As educators, we know already that achievement is inherently part of a human-centred approach. Achievement is a key aspect of how we grow and develop as individuals. On the one hand it motivates us by demonstrating the validity of our inner drive to belong, to fulfil our potential and to do good and right in the world. On the other hand, the successful negotiation of recognised pathways to success can also satisfy our need for external reward and recognition.

Achievement – and, particularly in the context of schools, student achievement – needs to be referenced against something for it to have currency and relevance. This will ultimately need to be a set of values, and it is preferable that these values are explicit and well understood within the school setting. A school therefore needs to have a value set that is important to the members of its community. It also needs some way of aligning community, team, family and individual expectations about what students should achieve and how that achievement will be influenced through the educational work of its community of inquiry and practice. The best way to do this in a school is by communicating to our stakeholders the standards, expectations and aspirations for achievement that we use to challenge, support and inspire growth. In establishing shared practice, we can align vision to intentions to actions to outputs – something that is done best when these are linked clearly to the graduate outcomes of the school or team within the school context.

So, whether we are talking about specific fields of activity, such as academic or co-curricular endeavour linked to graduate outcomes and external qualifications, or the development of character, competency, and wellness more broadly, we know we are making progress best when we set goals, direct activity towards the achievement of these goals and measure our success in respect to these goals. Without our goals we can have no yardstick to focus the intrinsic and extrinsic motivation of individuals or teams, no way of knowing whether effort and energy are being directed with the desired effect and no understanding of how well we are achieving our purpose.

Leaders also need to have the character and competency to manage how individual staff members influence student achievement and how a team responds to the imperative to promote achievement in the overall context of their school ecosystem. This requires, at a minimum, building an understanding of the capabilities of their organisation to support student achievement and implement its plans for improvement of staff capacity in this respect at personal, team and organisational levels. For an inexperienced member of staff, personal self-efficacy and student-achievement strategies may present challenges that require considerable personal and professional growth – though some less experienced teachers find these challenges relatively straightforward and can capitalise on their natural focus on the currency of holistic achievement. For experienced staff, the challenge is to continue to develop their own character, competency and wellness as part of a team in which they can contribute their adaptive expertise to projects connected to student achievement that might be otherwise beyond the influence of individual effort or focus. For leaders within a school, the challenge becomes one of assisting others across the whole organisation to develop their adaptive expertise and self-efficacy.

Of course, the context of a school and its students will determine what goals might be appropriate. As Vishal Talreja, co-founder of Dream a Dream in Bengaluru, India, explains, every leader must recognise how the specific needs of learners operate within the social contract of a learning community and how effectively that social contract adopts a disposition towards improving what happens in an educational setting to prepare learners to flourish in their world.

### GAME CHANGER INSIGHT

*'What we realised very early on was that while [our learners] had access to basic needs (food, clothing, shelter – even basic access to public education) none of it was really preparing them for success in the future. Their life trajectory was more or less decided for them, and no one was really helping them transition into a very different future. So that's what we started working on. We said if we create learning opportunities for these children where they learn a set of life skills like problem-solving, decision-making, managing conflict, looking and collaboration abilities to adapt and respond to the complexities and uncertainties of life, they might have a better chance to talk about their own future.'*

**Vishal Talreja**

Disciplined and purposeful practice, therefore, does not operate in a vacuum. It is always about its operation within a social context, its capacity to satisfy the requirements of the social contract in which it is engaged and its impact on the lives of people. It is also about how we build a culture that supports bringing both values and value to the good people we are trying to strengthen.

### ⑾ ENCOUNTER AND RESPOND

How might you measure the nature and success of your disciplined and purpose-driven practice in your school as a leader who strengthens achievement in the teams and the organisations that you serve?

# HOW CAN I BEST SERVE OTHERS?

## Selfless: The approach of leaders who strengthen

In many ways, as we have seen already in this chapter, it is the circumstances in which we find ourselves and our responses to them that will define our capacity to show the leadership that strengthens. There are many specific qualities and behaviours, exhibited by great leaders across a wide variety of contexts, that will help us to build teams and schools that are disciplined and purposeful in their pursuit of today's learning for tomorrow's world. We are sure you will already understand that in seeking to strengthen learning, culture, leadership and performance in a school, great leaders focus on the people (particularly the students), place, purpose and practice of a learning community – not the ambitions of the leader. The character of good people, after all, is all about selflessness, not selfishness.

This does not mean that leaders neglect themselves along the way. We can be of less or even no benefit to our community if we do not ensure that we are the best versions of ourselves that we can be. Fundamentally, though, how we influence, inspire, direct and motivate our teams to fulfil a purpose comes down to the attitude of those we are leading – how willing they are to learn, live, lead and work individually and together towards this purpose. Team attitude is so often the result of the personal qualities of leaders. There are four specific qualities we wish to emphasise the importance of in this respect: calmness, perseverance, passion and optimism.

### Calmness and perseverance

As leaders, we can build individual and collective discipline by being calm and by persevering. We need to seek to understand and be interested in team members while also insisting on high standards. We need to maintain good communication and be fair and consistent in our dealings with others. We need to be able to choose to hold on and see things through, so long as we have weighed up the benefits and consequences of steering a steady course.

How we demonstrate a calm, rational and controlled demeanour has a direct relationship to a team's capacity to learn from and display the same qualities in times of difficulty, crisis or panic, whether these are real or perceived. Managing emotions to remain calm and persevere in public contexts is therefore an essential skill for leaders, although it is also important to find ways to process and diffuse those emotions in a more private space. Resilience requires support and is rarely, if ever, a solo experience.

While we try to be calm and persevere, we need to recognise and acknowledge that leadership can be tough. Great leaders know that the real struggle is often not against others but against our own selves – our fear of failure and our apprehension that we just cannot do it. For those who find themselves contemplating something new this can be a daunting prospect. We can find ourselves inadvertently assenting to mediocrity when we opt to stay in the position we are familiar with rather than embrace the challenge. Playing it safe, following the rules – that seems like the best way to avoid failure. Alas, that pattern is awfully dangerous. So, how do we explain failure? Do we seek to make excuses, to blame others for our own shortcomings? Do we make light of ambition and pretend that it doesn't matter? Do we give up and find something else to do? Or, having set goals and worked towards them, do we instead accept that what we did on this occasion was just not good enough for our team? Do we learn the lessons of our defeat? If we have been doing something the same way, without success, do we keep on doing it? Or do we try something different? Do we make a new plan?

As leaders, we must do what we can to keep calm and persevere. Often it is the moments of struggle that unlock the answers and opportunities for growth, both personally and for the communities that we serve. And, if we want to make a difference, game-changing leadership calls on us to never wait for just the right time, because that time will never arrive.

Thus, we need to remember that both calmness and perseverance are qualities that can be learned. While the work we do as leaders may differ at times from that done by the rest of our teams, we must be prepared to model the standard of control, diligence, the courage to try, and the same self-discipline that we also require of them. We set the tone and standard. Standards become habits; habits become culture. We can become more proficient in exercising this approach with experience. In this way, the capacity to maintain a measured, professional approach in times of stress is also a by-product of the quality of professional learning, growth and development in which you and your team will have been engaged. We need to encourage and design such learning experiences for our team members to help them to reflect on their learning and grow in the strength they will in turn pass on to others.

### Passion and optimism

While calmness and perseverance drive discipline, purpose is often the by-product of passion and optimism. Leadership born of these qualities encourages a positive and enthusiastic team attitude that generates belief and commitment to the cause. By contrast, leadership without this energy and belief in who we are, where we are and what matters to us often results in negativity, cynicism and mistrust. Game-changing leadership that strengthens a community also benefits from foresight. Foresight is our ability to accurately predict future outcomes with optimism and hope. It is a long-term, bigger picture perspective on how certain events will unfold over a period of time – and how we can act to influence outcomes.

Geoff Southworth's (2009) seminal study on effective leaders in schools notes that the most successful school leaders tend to be highly optimistic people. Optimism is all about having a positive outlook, maintaining a sense of humour and developing long-term hope. Hope in the face of uncertainty and anxiety is a mark of excellence. This hope is held despite the tenor of immediate events, even if things seem hopeless. Hope is our passionate belief that we can – and we must – provide the best education for every student and the highest outcomes for every learner in our care. Above all, we must translate this hope from intent to action.

Where should this action and our passion for it be directed? Given our own context as leaders in schools, principal of Camberwell Girls Grammar School in Victoria Debbie Dunwoody argues we need the passion to help others in our learning communities to connect with their own purpose and passion for continuous learning and unlearning, and individual and collective growth. After all, learning is our core business. If we aren't passionate about it and about the potential of all of our students and staff to learn, then we are in the wrong business!

## GAME CHANGER INSIGHT

*'I think, for me, it's really important that one of the purposes is about helping to enable and develop a passion for learning, because for all of us, we need to be lifelong learners.'*

**Debbie Dunwoody**

So much of the tone and environment of a team that underpins successful team culture, therefore, depends on our own attitude. It's about the positive and healthy disposition that we display towards ourselves, our teams and the call to learn, live, lead and work together. Leaders help their teams see the way forward. So much of this has positive thinking as its foundation.

The hardest part of being passionate about our work is having the confidence to believe in ourselves, especially when everything seems to be going against us.

It is human and natural for us to have doubts. However, though expressing vulnerability or uncertainty in the short term is reasonable, the job of the leader who strengthens is not to dwell publicly on indecision, anxiety or even dress-rehearse tragedy. Even when team members seem to be opposed to us or there are other frustrations that are not of our making, it is possible for us to move forward with passion for our purpose and the practice that flows from it because that passion is grounded in a deep appreciation of our people and our place.

So, we should never stop being passionate for and about our people. They are our greatest asset. When we complement our passion and optimism with calmness and perseverance, these key qualities balance to genuinely strengthen a community of inquiry and practice that has the energy and commitment to build today's learning for tomorrow's world.

> **ENCOUNTER AND RESPOND**
>
> We invite you to encounter and respond to a process of thinking differently about selfless leadership:
>
> - What does being selfless as a leader look like in your school? What *should* it look like in your school? Respond by collecting a series of images and keywords, which may also include original drawings and text, that best articulate your vision for high performance.
> - What could it mean to think differently about leading selflessly in your context? What kinds of changes can you make to your leadership practice to support this?

## WHOSE AM I?

Leaders strengthen the character and achievement of their school communities by using their own character to add to the character capital of their school and build its culture. We enhance the purpose and disciplined achievement of our teams, demonstrating the qualities of calmness, perseverance, passion and optimism. This is how we make the values and value propositions of our schools most apparent.

> **(II) ENCOUNTER AND RESPOND**
>
> Are you a leader who strengthens? We invite you to encounter the following reflective questions and respond to them by identifying two to three priorities for your own professional learning and the growth of your adaptive expertise and self-efficacy in building culture:
>
> - How do I strengthen the values and value proposition of my school by modelling, scaffolding and coaching using my leadership practices and relationships?
> - How do I strengthen the capacity of my school's learning opportunities to support students' growth in character, competency and wellness?
> - How do I strengthen the priority given to student agency, voice and advocacy within my school's academic, co-curricular and pastoral programs?
> - How do I strengthen school character, culture and climate by monitoring, repairing and shaping pathways for each student to develop a sense of belonging and to be supported to make progress and succeed in my school's articulated graduate outcomes?
> - How do I strengthen operational systems and structures by connecting them to my school's stated ethos and purpose?

Strengthening is always about change. Right now, we are, as a profession, changing ourselves. We are changing our work. We are changing how we connect with and support the whole education of our students and their families. We need to be able to co-construct a compelling narrative that helps school members to understand where the journey is taking them and why it is necessary for them to join the collective and determined enterprise. As leaders do the work of strengthening, they also need to think through how they share their purpose with their community and help to forge a narrative of change and continuity across yesterday, today and tomorrow in a future-fit school. In the next chapter, we will explore the competency of leaders who inform.

# CHAPTER 3
# Leadership that informs

## FUTURE READY AND FUTURE FIT: INTRODUCING LEADERSHIP THAT INFORMS

We live in a rapidly changing world. The volume, pace and intensity of our times mean that we need to be able to respond to change readily and willingly. We need to be ready for the things that life throws at us, navigate our way through complexity and enjoy the good fortune with which we are blessed. In this context, as leaders in schools, we need to understand where we are leading our communities and how to help them get there. In doing this future-building leadership work we inform. We need to cultivate a shared understanding of the context, trajectory and sense of our community of inquiry and practice. We need to work with the community to develop and share a compelling narrative of future builders through creating and communicating a vision of a preferred future.

So, what might this shared future be? Madeleine Grummet, investor at Startmate and SheEO™, journalist, and host of the *Human Cogs* podcast, speaks of a deep understanding of the future-fit character, competency and wellness of thriving and the conditions under which it might be grown.

> **GAME CHANGER INSIGHT**
>
> 'So, the purpose of schooling here ... is to produce the next generation who will come up with the innovations and solutions that will drive the engines of our future economy and our future society ... When we look at some of the huge issues that we're facing in society ... young people are stepping into a completely different world and context. And so there's an urgency about the world and the sorts of problems that they're inheriting. And I think the role of education is to ensure that those young people, their talents and energy are harnessed as best as possible so they can step in and become the caretakers of Australia and the world into the future.'
>
> — Madeleine Grummet

Our global research tells us that every individual and every school community needs to have a clear understanding of a compelling narrative that takes them from yesterday to today to tomorrow. By ensuring that your shared sense of purpose is future fit in the way that Grummet recommends, you can align, connect and drive all of the decision-making in your school to design and deliver what we believe is the new social contract of education: today's learning for tomorrow's world. You can house education, culture, leadership and performance within a dynamic learning ecosystem that is future fit in character: deeply human centred; technologically enriched; people, place and planet conscious; and intentionally purposeful.

This is a big step forward and up for most schools. As a game changer, you will need to bring people with you. You will need to use leadership that informs you to secure the willingness and commitment of your community to go on this journey and tell this narrative together. You'll need to use authentic and credible persuasion as to why your sense of the future should become a shared sense, and why this sense should in turn become a shared vision for a preferred future. It won't be enough simply to bombard people with detail. You'll need to help them to see what lies ahead and how to build the voice, agency and advocacy of individuals, teams and the community as a whole – all of which will be required to navigate the journey ahead with success.

In this chapter we look at leadership that informs using the same four-step, inside-out process of leadership development. In posing the question 'Who am I?'

we will explore the character and purpose of leaders who inform by crafting a vision and building leadership while demonstrating the graduate outcome of future builders. We will answer the question 'Where do I fit in?' by outlining a toolkit for practice based on the fundamentals of communication and persuasion. We will reflect on how sharing vision through a distributed approach to leadership concentrating on delegation, supervision and feedback can help us to answer the question 'How can I best serve others?' Finally, you will have the opportunity to respond to the question 'Whose am I?' by thinking through how to bring your own value to your school community through leadership that informs.

# WHO AM I?

## Future builders: The character of leaders who inform

As future builders, how might we direct our leadership towards formulating, articulating and implementing a vision? A vision, in a technical sense, is a statement of a realistic, credible and preferred future for a school. This vision can provide the direction that equips leaders and their teams with the knowledge of where they are now, where they are going, the means to get there and the desired end state. Leslie Medema, head of learning at Green School International, makes clear to us, vision needs to have aspiration at its core.

### GAME CHANGER INSIGHT

'A school like ours is needed today because we are not capitalising on the abilities and diversity and beauty of the minds of all of the children. So most programs and exams will only prioritise one type of knowledge. And the reality is, where is that really entrepreneurial child? Where is that really artistic child? Where is that person who doesn't fit into that standard body of knowledge? Where is their outlet and where is the ability of our teachers and our systems – actually, our teachers are doing this all the time – but our systems, to recognise that actually that is what we need for the future is all different kinds of thinkers, all working together, but all wanting to make a positive impact as well, having that drive to make a positive impact.'

Leslie Medema

School leaders need to be thinking about aspirations such as these and using them to form a vision that can act as both the rationale and the articulation of how this vision will be realised within their school (or team within their school). The development of a vision statement will help them to achieve this.

What does a vision statement do? A vision statement helps to articulate a vision (where we want to go together) and enable the development of the purpose and values (why we want to go there) that will inform strategy (how we get there) and guide the team culture and behaviours that will help to bring the vision to life (what we need to do, individually and together).

What does a vision statement look like? A vision statement must inevitably include the values of the school to which it belongs. It must be aimed at describing and realising a preferred future. It should be action oriented, focused on how to bring this preferred future about. Such statements should challenge, create, focus, inspire and commit teams. They should be short and easily understood. They need to be ambitious and invoke a lasting mental picture that feels distinctive or even unique while fitting the needs of the larger group, organisation or community.

How might leaders who inform translate this vision from theory into action? Having defined a vision together with their community, a leader needs to ensure they share and articulate this vision effectively among their teams regularly and consistently. Alignment with vision is perhaps the most important fundamental behaviour for all members of a future-fit school community: they need to agree on the 'where', 'why', 'how' and 'what'. It may be very challenging to build complete alignment. Game changers who inform need to use their leadership to develop a critical mass of support for the essence of our vision: what really matters. We need to become experts at saying what this is and building it into our daily discourse. Jonathan McIntosh, chief academic officer of Prospect Schools in the United States, is very clear about the vision for Prospect Schools' students.

### GAME CHANGER INSIGHT

*'We're a school that believes implicitly and explicitly in the power of a diverse student body that really represents the communities that our schools are serving.'*

Jonathan McIntosh

Members of a school community will need to make a choice about their adherence to such a vision, but it's hard to argue against logic such as this if they choose to be part of the community, especially when it reminds all of what we are here to do: improve more outcomes for learners in keeping with the values and value propositions of our schools.

Vision can and should develop over time as resources and ideas change. To manage this effectively, make sure that you institute processes of review and, if necessary, realigning the team or community with emerging changes to your vision. Leaders need to continually interpret and explain, review and reinforce this vision in the context of their own teams so that it stays relevant and engaging for team members and strengthens their connection with the broader school community.

In this way, the process of revision becomes one of renewal in which we can encourage practitioners to continue to step forward and up into the future. We can help them to re-examine both our and their purpose as educators and test that purpose against their understanding of the needs of people, place and planet. We can help them to see how this plays out in their practice. This is where we provide students with a rich and full proving ground that acts as a transition from childhood to adulthood, a space that calls for exploration, encounter and discovery in which learners rehearse for success as adults in a world where the need for adaptive expertise and self-efficacy is matched by the need for courage and compassion.

Thus, the character of future builders, the second graduate outcome of a school for tomorrow, balances consultation, clarity and advocacy for a meaningful perspective about the state of the human condition and the role of education in advancing it.

## Learn

Future builders want to be leaders for the future. Inspired by authenticity, they have the reflectiveness, sensitivity and strength to manage complexity by honouring the legacy of yesterday, attending to the needs of today and looking forward to what tomorrow will require of them.

## Live

They are willing to become dedicated leaders who translate vision into a shared story of progress and human endeavour. While many leaders, including some in our schools and educational systems, just concentrate on the operational demands of the present, future builders dream of tomorrow. They honour yesterday and attend to today while simultaneously getting up onto a balcony to see beyond the immediacy of the horizon to what living, learning, leading and working tomorrow might look like. They use patience, judgement and insight to build a narrative that helps them to forge a path towards this preferred future and take others on the journey. They justify what their teams need to do and how it should be done.

### Lead

They seek to communicate effectively. They understand that communication competency involves explaining the complexity that is at the heart of leadership for the future by constructing compelling narratives for continuity and change over yesterday, today and tomorrow. This relies on the capacity to address different audiences and purposes with clear and accurate expression that is well-informed, reliable and persuasive.

### Work

They are grounded in learning about narrative, which helps them to acquire knowledge of how to motivate, influence and direct the actions of others towards achieving a willingly shared goal; gain skills in communicating with others about the object and subject of their leadership mission; nurture a disposition towards maintaining a focus or holding the line on a long-term vision; and build the capacity to reflect on how they use their communication to speak to complexity.

## Building leadership: The purpose of leaders who inform

We believe that it's our job as leaders who inform to locate ourselves simultaneously at the head and in the middle of our communities. We need to build leadership at all levels in our schools, especially among our students, so that we graduate future builders who are themselves strong, compassionate and future-ready leaders who are also adept communicators.

Schools, therefore, need leaders who are focused significantly on the future of their community. They need to apply models and frameworks of positive leadership that balance honouring the past and addressing the demands of the present while prioritising looking forward to a preferred future. Through their communication they share a narrative of their school's growth and development as a future-focused school. They manage complexity in their leadership by listening to their school community carefully, connecting and communicating with it, and creating a credible story of the progress of the school that honours the legacy of its past, frames the requirements of its present and projects a compelling rationale for a preferred future that is best served by authentic learning experiences based on character, competency and wellness.

Through their different communication functions, they help their community to come along with them on their journey. They are energised by deliberate, targeted and intentional approaches to community engagement that are informed by an understanding of both the relationships between needs and wants of stakeholders and what their school promises and delivers on an ongoing basis in building a school for the future. They talk about and report on their work consistently and with quality. They connect with their community and engage the progress of their work towards their preferred future through effective communication and reporting.

Leaders in contemporary school communities spend a lot of time listening to those around them. This process of consultation is an essential element of any communication function. There is an expectation that all stakeholders have voices that need to be heard, although these will not always be agreed with and acted upon. All of us need to be given clarity at times and sometimes it is the role of a leader to make decisions about why we do what we do and how we are going to get there. Sometimes we can misread the tone required for this – firm, strong leadership can often be mistaken for arrogance. Balancing this need to provide direction and instruction while remaining approachable and relational in tone is an interesting issue for leaders in schools. Humility and willpower can be seen as opposite poles. Yet, as business leader and writer Jim Collins (2001) explains in *Good to Great*, great leaders know that it is possible to resolve and bridge what can often feel like irreconcilable tension between these two qualities. In other words, one can be a genuine leader who directs their team with care and consideration as a servant, listening closely to views and humbly taking feedback, while also staying strong to the purpose and vision for the future. You will need the right character and a clear set of guiding principles to do this well – being a servant leader who puts the needs of others first does not mean being a pushover!

We also need to be careful that our leadership that informs also takes us somewhere meaningful and substantive. We need to help our school communities to think about both their compelling reasons why, as well as the 'how' and 'what' that will make this rationale real for learners, teachers and families. We suggest that this advocacy needs to champion a vision of today's learning for tomorrow's world. It needs to argue the case for educators to equip, empower and enable students, teachers, leaders and school teams with the adaptive expertise, emotional competency and self-efficacy to make active contributions towards our individual and collective futures.

Yong Zhao, distinguished professor in the School of Education at the University of Kansas and now also professor in the Graduate School of Education at the University of Melbourne argues passionately and convincingly for his vision for education that is about the whole person in their context. He calls on us to transcend a simplified transactional process of testing and pathways to consider the transformation of the potential of individuals and groups.

> **GAME CHANGER INSIGHT**
>
> *'I believe all societies are created by human beings and there are certain things that can be changed, and we should create our people to be better social constructors.'*
>
> Yong Zhao

A school informed by this sense of social responsibility demonstrates a shared understanding of the needs of its students. Students need to know what they are learning – that's aspiration. They need to go on a journey of encounter, connection, challenge and discovery to acquire character and competencies – that's experience. They need to join us as the co-authors of the narrative of this learning journey – that's agency. They need to discover their own identity and how best to express it through their learning and relationships – that's voice. And they need to be provided with the time, support and conditions that will help them to make the most of their learning – that's resource.

Such a school sees its capacity growing along pathways or corridors that are defined by its graduate outcomes, the stages of which are measured according to a learning community's maturity model that assesses its journey to become fit for purpose. In doing all of these things, an excellent school becomes replete with the education, culture, leadership and performance to develop the necessary character, competency and wellness. This equips, empowers and enables students on The Pathway to Excellence to acquire the adaptive expertise, emotional competency and self-efficacy required for them to flourish in their world. It earns the right to call itself a school for tomorrow. This is the standard that we as game changers encourage our communities of inquiry and practice to adopt as we pursue the job of improving outcomes for our learners.

To create and advocate for the potential of a future-ready and future-fit education to help society as a whole, game changers need to be able to gather a school around a bold vision and use it to help its members to take the big step forward and up. Typically, community involvement should make this process function more smoothly, but almost always this will not happen exactly as we might wish. Effective communication is often the necessary step in bridging the gap between the intention for change and action taken to make it happen. We need to ensure that what we are doing individually and also together as a whole educational enterprise is focused on achieving what we perceive to be our shared purpose. We also need people to understand why we are choosing to take action to bring our values and value propositions to our communities instead of simply doing things the way they have always been done.

To do this, we need to weave together a compelling narrative of today's learning for tomorrow's world. We also need to understand that not everything needs to be about change all of the time. The status quo within the story of yesterday, today and tomorrow is often a shrewd starting point for any community. Wise leaders will be quick to identify the useful customs and honourable traditions that should be maintained and nurtured. They need to recognise the difference between advocacy for continuity and advocacy for change – and know how to balance the two.

## ENCOUNTER AND RESPOND
What is your own model of purpose and practice as a leader who informs?

# WHERE DO I FIT IN?

## The practice of a leader who informs

Much has been said about communication in schools. In our global consulting practice at a School for tomorrow. we often find that schools and their leaders are criticised more frequently for the quality, consistency and effectiveness of their communication than for any other domain of school life. It's a constant process to work out that Goldilocks factor: not too much and not too little so that it's just right. All schools, the people within them and especially their leaders need to be proactive in providing accurate and supportive communication. They also need to take care with the brand of a school and its particular visual identity. This relates strongly to – and flows from – alignment of the community with the vision of the school. The more connected and informed people are, the more likely it is that their own communication will be supportive and constructive.

Leaders communicate through their words, presence, standards, actions and behaviours. They manage reporting. They also support the development and implementation of a vision through their capacity to persuade their community of the validity of this vision and its relevance for students, staff and their families.

Having worked with school leaders in communities all around the world we are able to suggest a set of common leadership practices centred on the fundamentals of communication and persuasion of leaders who inform. These are articulated for leaders at both team and organisational levels in tables 3.1 and 3.2 respectively.

### Table 3.1: Informing as a leader of a team

| | |
|---|---|
| **FUNDAMENTALS OF COMMUNICATION** | Employs effective verbal and non-verbal communication to inform, motivate and control the team and to express appropriate emotions. |
| | Provides responsible, accurate, brief and clear written communication that promotes the team's credibility and the mission's viability. |
| | Demonstrates effective listening and speaking skills with team members. |
| **PERSUASION** | Communicates to the team a clear vision that challenges, creates, focuses and commits the team. |
| | Successfully translates the vision into action through positive leadership. |
| | Continually interprets, reviews and reinforces the team vision. |

### Table 3.2: Informing as a leader of an organisation

| | |
|---|---|
| **FUNDAMENTALS OF COMMUNICATION** | Demonstrates superior interpersonal sensitivity. |
| | Displays high-level written and oral communication skills. |
| **PERSUASION** | Conceptualises the ethos and purpose of the school, creates a compelling vision to achieve this purpose and relates organisational and team structures and work to these concepts and vision. |
| | Inspires the organisation and its teams with the agreed vision and focuses their actions intently and passionately on the enterprise of making this happen. |

## The fundamentals of communication and reporting

Communication serves at least five important functions for you as a leader: informing, motivating, directing, persuading and expressing emotion. Effective communication also institutes, develops and improves relationships between team members. Your leadership communication refers to the written and spoken word, and any other activity – intentional or unintentional – used by you to affect the culture of a school, the achievement of its strategy and the embedding of this strategy into the daily life of that school and the behaviours of its stakeholders. It is, in many ways, the most important tool of your leadership. Without adequate contact, connection and communication, it is difficult to establish a positive influence, develop sound relationships or get the job done.

Interpersonal communication, therefore, is really important in our context as game changers. It requires patience and persistence as we move among the team, reminding them of the goal, the need for its completion and the standard to which it must be achieved, as well as advising on how this might all be done. In this way, with some judicious people management and an ever-present attention to detail, you might prevent your good intentions from coming to nothing, instead getting the desired job done and moving everyone steadily towards a preferred future.

Listening is probably the most important part of the communication process. People care passionately about education and children and they will want to express their opinions. We know that everyone has had an experience of education themselves and will be drawing on that experience to inform these opinions with a greater or lesser degree of expertise. Quite often, when they seek intervention and do not get the decision they want, people will criticise the communication process, but most likely they just want and need to be heard; they will judge your leadership by how well you listen, even if you do not always give them the result they want.

In this context especially, the substance of what you communicate is important – but remember the form and tone of your communication usually carries more weight than your words. This means that the way you sound and the way you look can have more impact than the actual words you use. Leaders therefore need to always be conscious of their body language and the message this communicates, both as they speak and as they listen. This is one of the reasons why a leader must always present well. Dress and bearing are critical in this; the way you look and the way you carry yourself communicates much about your standards. If you look as though you care about yourself and your role, then you will have a much better chance of convincing your team that you are an appropriate role model.

A traditional term we use to describe another application of communication in schools is reporting. A school and the members of its community can communicate and report on many aspects of school performance, including programs and people. A school reports for many reasons. Reporting is as important to the core role of the new teacher as it is to the chair of the school board. Clearly, they will be reporting about different things and they will probably be using different means, but what they will share is the reality that the activity is a key part of their roles. One of the most important features of any communications reporting activity within a school is the development of a culture of accuracy. A significant and ongoing challenge in building a positive culture of communication with a school community is therefore to help all community members to communicate with each other in a way that is simple, clear, fair and effective.

## Persuasion

The case that needs to be put in favour of today's learning for tomorrow's world and its connection with the future of your school is an important one. It is a story of an education that frees others to locate their authentic voice, agency and advocacy through the growth and development of their character, competency and wellness. As individuals learn, live, lead and work in this way, the whole ecosystem that supports their thriving is itself liberated from the constraints of compliance. This allows its operations to work towards its aspiration for excellence that respects the desire for all of us to become the best versions of ourselves. As Dr Kasonde Musoma, director of leadership and character formation at the Tecnológico de Monterrey in Mexico, notes, a future-fit education frees learners to become the people they need to be.

> **GAME CHANGER INSIGHT**
>
> *'I have three Ps that I tell all my students. The first P is I hope that in the process of education, you find a place of passion. I hope that in the process of your education, you find your place of purpose. And I hope that when in the process of education, you find your place of power ... I believe the education of the future and the education that I hope that as game changers we're speaking to is an education that liberates.'*
>
> Dr Kasonde Musoma

If you agree with this, then you are ready to become a game changer through leadership that informs.

As a starting point, your basic communication skills can become the glue that binds communities together. You can also be the facilitator for communications and reporting systems that connect the stories of learners to the people around them. Further to this, you can step forward and up into your persuasive function by advocating for a process of iterative improvement through continuity and change that will lead to the realisation of your vision for a preferred future. You can also be a broker that helps the conflict of apparently contradictory views to become reconciled and synthesised into a single shared vision or methodology of practice.

You will need to try your best, as a team or organisational leader, to ensure those you work with are able to communicate about and act in alignment with the ethos, purpose and culture of the school and its articulation in the form of a clear vision for a preferred future. Throughout the whole process of defining and implementing a vision you should not be shy about consulting your team. It's expected in our times that teams and their members will have at least some voice and agency in the process, as well as the opportunity to advocate for what they believe is right. In this respect, it's probably better to think of an organisation – particularly a school and its community – as a network with hubs, spokes and connections rather than as a hierarchy. Everybody shares the same responsibility for the speed, accuracy, supportiveness, connectivity and consistency of messaging about what matters to all of the community. The specific roles and responsibilities of different community members within this network will vary; some will be instrumental in establishing a vision, while others may help to shape it and outline the elements of its implementation through a series of important planning documents, but all will have a responsibility to endorse and work towards implementing it.

If you can appreciate this, you can ensure that your thinking about a preferred future and the roles of others in helping to bring it about does not unfold in isolation from the experiences, expectations, and professional and personal ambitions of your team. This will require you to ensure that the whole process of communication is in accord, particularly when working together to build plans for the future. In this respect, we encourage leaders to use the a School for tomorrow. 5D approach:

- Discover the most relevant data about the school and/or team journey and its stakeholders' sense of belonging and connection to the actual educational experience of the school.
- Diagnose the patterns you are seeing in the data, which will allow you to tell a true story of yesterday, today and tomorrow.
- Decide what needs to be done to create a preferred future and the strategy to build it.
- Design a solution for reaching the preferred future together. This includes the likely steps required to make this happen, the desired culture that will support the achievement of these steps and the shape and character of the ecosystem that will house this culture.
- Deploy a range of plans and initiatives that will define the key milestones and the flow of daily life in key areas of operations as the community proceeds toward making its vision happen.

## ⏸ ENCOUNTER AND RESPOND

How might you measure the nature and success of your communication and persuasion practice in your school as a leader who informs in both the teams and the organisations in which you serve?

# HOW CAN I BEST SERVE OTHERS?

## Distributed: The approach of leaders who inform

Distribution is the way in which we share the work of building the future of a preferred future together. Sharing the responsibility for leadership and its essential communication functions is a way of maintaining both direction and momentum in an organisation that achieves high-quality results while encouraging people who are working within it to show their own leadership and initiative.

You will do this formally through working with your team to develop goals that are linked directly to your vision statement as well as plans to achieve these goals. You will review progress with your team at least monthly, and sometimes even weekly, to ensure that you stay on track. You will need courage to ensure that your shared vision for a preferred future maintains its integrity and meets the needs of the school community without being compromised by the urgency of the present.

This type of distributed and relational approach to a team's communication as they implement a vision is essential to the role of a game changer who informs. It involves developing confidence in exercising two specific leadership functions: delegating responsibility to others, then providing supervision and feedback during implementation.

### Delegation

Delegation is an approach to structuring a shared responsibility for leadership. In our context, this is to achieve a set of goals that contribute towards a common purpose using the constraints presented and the boundaries of a school's strategy and agreed culture. In suitable situations, delegation can allow team members to grow their competencies, bring their own perspectives to the generation of solutions and demonstrate their own personality and way of doing things. It is not appropriate in every instance, but you should find it very useful in a wide range of scenarios and team tasks.

First you will need to deliver a brief to your team. A brief is where you give instructions that will focus people on the purpose, needs and execution of a task at hand in some detail, making sure that they understand what they need to achieve, the standard necessary and why. This is different from a brainstorming suggestion, which is a structured opportunity for a group to throw ideas around and develop potential solutions. Instead, a brief will usually involve a brief summary of the context, an overview of the essential work that needs to be done, what success might look like when the work is complete, the timelines within which the team will need to operate and the essential resources at hand to get the job done.

Part of the skill in using this approach and structure is in applying it consistently so that team members know what to expect with how you communicate your expectations to them. You should aim to write down your brief in advance and deliver it from the written copy. It is also wise to ask team members to write it down as you are giving it or provide them with a copy. How you use questions to test understanding among the team at the end of the brief is critical – it allows you to see what your team has taken on board and whether they are ready to begin working on the task.

From here, the responsibility for designing and implementing a plan should be delegated to the team members. Ask the team to identify their ideas for how they will achieve their individual and group tasks. Listen to and validate their suggestions, then add your own input only if it is necessary. When you arrive at a solution, make sure that this is written down and that team members have a copy.

### Supervision and feedback

Once your team has a clear idea of their roles and responsibilities within the plan, you need to allow them to get on with it while you supervise and provide feedback. As a general principle, you can't do the jobs of the members of your team. Your job is to lead them, not to shield them from their own work or to be overly specific or overbearing in directing them about how to perform their roles. Most teams do not like to be micromanaged outside of new, dangerous or technically complex situations.

It is difficult to supervise when you are not there to observe what is happening, but you must also resist the temptation to become too involved. Watch carefully what team members are doing. While they are engaged in the task, ask questions to see how they are going and what further support they need. Allow them to feel that they have been seen and heard, that you value their work, that they are in control of their own processes as they work within the group's joint determination and agreed plan. Zeina Chalich, principal consultant at Learning Creatives Consultancy, notes that your aim needs to be to affirm what your team is doing well and to steer them back on track when they are struggling.

> **GAME CHANGER INSIGHT**
>
> *'When people feel acknowledged and affirmed and seen and heard and valued, they have purpose in their work and they bring their whole selves to whatever they're doing.'*
>
> — Zeina Chalich

So, you need to offer constructive criticism and affirm when the team is making progress. When something is working well, acknowledge it and hold the conversation there for a moment to explore it further before you move on to what's next. Avoid the 'praise sandwich' of a positive followed by a negative followed by a positive in the same conversation – otherwise, every time you offer a compliment they will expect the opposite to follow shortly after. Instead, to encourage and provide a sense of momentum, use confirmation of the attainment of a series of predicted and significant milestones as well as observations about unexpected outcomes that add value to the process.

Consider carefully how you might intervene when team members make mistakes. A tactful approach designed to strengthen their skills is always appreciated. Sometimes it is also better to allow team members the opportunity to work through their errors themselves with little or no prompting from you. This will allow them to develop their own problem-solving skills and make them less dependent on you for every detail. Be aware, though, that you will sometimes need to become very involved, especially when your team is new or lacking in the skills required to achieve a task, or when the outcomes are very different to what was needed.

When you see something going wrong, think about using it as a teaching moment. At this point, you need to remember that it is always better to teach the team how to do something than to do it for them. Think about asking people to explain what they have done and why they have done it before offering judgement. Try to help them see that there are usually other options and perhaps talk them through how to generate solutions that might achieve better results. Ask them to commit to change and then notice and comment on that change when you see it.

When you give feedback, make sure it is honest. Leaders in schools often avoid giving honest feedback because they do not wish to hurt their team members' feelings or to be confrontational. Hard conversations can be challenging, but how is your team going to know how well they have done and how much they need to improve if they receive only false praise and over encouragement? One way of solving this problem is using gentle language and tone when conveying underperformance. You can also ask teams to critique themselves first. You will usually find that they identify many problems themselves. Your role can then be to clarify the areas that need improvement, refine their understanding and then, most importantly, help them develop solutions. In this way, you can turn a potentially intimidating task into a constructive and positive process.

You also need to think about and balance the differing needs of the team, the task and the individuals involved. And remember that wellness comes first. It's just as important to attend to team members' physical contexts as it is to ensure that they are aligned in their purpose and practice with the strategy and culture of their school. Make sure your team members have adequate time for rest and relaxation, especially when engaging with longer tasks.

> ## ENCOUNTER AND RESPOND
>
> We invite you to encounter and respond to a process of thinking differently about distributed leadership:
>
> - What does delegation, supervision and feedback within distributed leadership look like in your school? What *should* it look like in your school? Respond by collecting images and keywords, which may also include original drawings and text, that best articulate your vision for high-performance.
>
> - What could it mean to think differently about distributing leadership in your context? What kinds of changes can you make to your leadership practice to support this?

## WHOSE AM I?

The journey of being and becoming for students in a school for tomorrow is the experience of gaining mastery of the adaptive expertise, emotional competency and self-efficacy required to thrive in their world. Their accomplishment is evidenced through attainment of their graduate outcomes. Our map of the experience of schooling must help our students chart the possible journeys to these outcomes and the acquisition of character, competency and wellness on The Pathway to Excellence. This must give our students the opportunity to develop their voice, agency and advocacy.

> ## (II) ENCOUNTER AND RESPOND
>
> Are you a leader who informs? We invite you to encounter the following reflective questions and respond to them by identifying two to three priorities for your own professional learning and the growth of your adaptive expertise and self-efficacy as a leader who informs:
>
> - How do I craft and tell a compelling story of my school's yesterday, today and tomorrow, communicating a vision for the future as a school fit for the purpose of educating young people in the character, competency and wellness they need to succeed and flourish in their world?
> - How do I create publications that inform my school community about the standards and behaviours necessary for the collective journey of change towards a co-created vision for the future?
> - How do I foster a language of high performance across my school through which everyone is supported in achieving the best possible outcomes for students?
> - How do I hold honest and courageous conversations in which I listen with empathy and then provide care, clarity and direction in my responses?
> - How do I strive to communicate with students with authenticity, respect and caring?

As leaders who inform we help to draw the map of this experience and encourage our teams and organisations to join with us to achieve the purpose for which they have been assembled. We want you to lead with vision and create a shared purpose within your school. In this chapter we have connected continuity and change to the fundamental and persuasive communications tasks of leaders who inform. So much of the success of this depends on how well leaders can orient their communities to transformation through continuous learning and help them find their bearings in this context. This is what we will turn our attention to next.

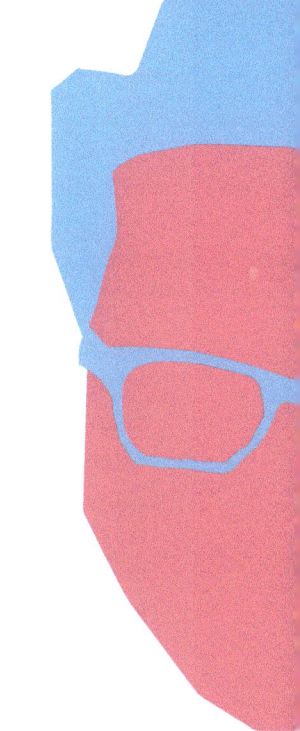

# CHAPTER 4
# Leadership that orientates

## TRANSFORMATION THROUGH CONTINUOUS LEARNING: INTRODUCING LEADERSHIP THAT ORIENTATES

As our world is transforming around us, we need to be open to undergoing a parallel and continuing process of transformation of ourselves, our students and our schools. What might once have worked for some in education as a series of content-heavy transactions on a pathway of social preferment and advancement is no longer appropriate for us all – it's neither future ready nor is it future fit.

A future-ready and future-fit learning culture means stepping forward into a preferred future where vision and vocabulary are shared; values and value propositions are agreed by the school community; and the velocity, shape and trajectory of change are designed and implemented to meet the needs of internal and external contexts. In this vein, we can't expect to build the right sort of learning through a single practice or set of practices in teaching or learning prescribed as 'the answer'. We therefore need to be agnostic to 'the right answer' and look instead to flexible and layered modes of curriculum, pedagogy and assessment practices that are connected to context and culture. All student learning journeys need to be formed within the context and culture of the transformation of the school community. We need to use evidence and research to validate that the choices we make about learning within a community are actually helping our learners to be transformed into future-ready and future-fit graduates.

This process of the transformation of students on their journeys and experiences of school should be enhanced by a shared commitment to continuous learning. Continuous learning is a flexible online and offline approach to the design, development and delivery of learning and teaching that allows all to access learning from their own location — anytime, anywhere, by anyone. Continuous learning does not prescribe a particular pedagogical approach. Rather, it supports the transformation of the learner through a combination of teacher-directed, student-centred and student-led approaches in the curriculum and co-curriculum. These approaches need to be both personalised and situated within the whole of learning. They need to promote the incremental acquisition of adaptive expertise and self-efficacy. They need to contribute to a process of progress and (ultimately) transformation of the individual through growth in the future-fit character, competency and wellness that will allow them to thrive in a world that is constantly shifting and demanding more from less.

A transformational education for character, competency and wellness occurs in every part of the school, is built through relationships, refined through specific pedagogies and propelled by the culture of the school. This education needs to be guided by a shared and agreed model of continuous learning, around which a community of inquiry and practice might be built according to design principles that encourage educators to plan, share, coach, measure, listen for, live, grow and defend it. Through a blend of explicit and implicit, deliberate and spontaneous pedagogies, educators must seek, above all, to grow the character of the whole person. This character and the competencies associated with it will be expressed in a set of graduate outcomes that indicate what sort of person the community wants to produce and how they will be ready to thrive in their world. These graduate outcomes will in turn shape the design and delivery of a framework for education for character, competency and wellness – a cascading set of documents that describe how learning will occur in all parts of the school, from vision to intention to means to results. All of this will be housed in a human-centred, technologically enriched and intentionally purposeful school ecosystem that is also people, place and planet conscious.

Relationships matter greatly within this ecosystem because people matter. We need to ensure that all learning opportunities that occur within it focus as much on the social and emotional growth of learners and their connections with others as they do on the development of their individual cognition and metacognition. Learning experiences need to allow multiple entry points for students to construct their learning through active engagement that leads to exploration, encounter and discovery. This calls for a mix of pedagogies, including guided and active approaches as well as inquiry-based and service learning. These need to occur within an environment that fosters self-directed learners who can develop metacognition, optimises the acquisition and transfer of knowledge and skills, supports the regulation of emotions in a safe and supportive context, manages study and planning, and sets higher personal and collective goals for learning attainment and growth.

In short, every learner needs to feel seen and valued in a continuous learning paradigm. The object of continuous learning is their transformation and the process of helping students become the best versions of themselves should move them from engagement to empowerment. It needs to shape and be shaped by learning experiences that enhance students' adaptive expertise and self-efficacy, build their growth in character, competency and wellness, increase their self-determination and also therefore augment their capacity to thrive in their world.

While we know that we need to place the transformation of learners at the centre of our model of continuous learning, at the same time, we need to recognise that teachers are the key agents of this transformation. As Yasodai Selvakumaran, finalist in the 2019 Global Teacher Prize, points out, this is where teaching starts for many of us.

### GAME CHANGER INSIGHT

*'It's just really inspiring knowing that we're contributing, not only to the lives of our students, which is often what gets people into teaching in the first place, and really making a difference in communities more broadly.'*

**Yasodai Selvakumaran**

In a similar vein, we believe that leading teaching towards the transformation of learners commits a whole school community of inquiry and practice to growth. This is characterised by how all community members model, scaffold and coach each other on behaviours based on self-efficacy and adaptive expertise in pursuit of the progressive attainment of iterative standards.

Leadership that promotes this draws on the capability of understanding and managing change. School leaders and governors share a responsibility for certifying that strategy, leadership, operations and governance within a school community are personalised to the needs of learners, aligned with the standards and expectations of that school community and society more broadly. They are also called to ensure that all of this is integrated in such a way that the values and value proposition of their school are clearly embedded through a framework for education based on the desired graduate outcomes. In short, when we orientate, we guide those travelling with us towards the purpose of our school and encourage them to connect this to their own sense of purpose.

In this chapter we look at the leadership competency of orientating and how leaders can orientate individuals, teams and learning organisations towards transformation through continuous learning. In 'Who am I?' we will explore the character and purpose of continuous learners and unlearners who build learning through reflection on the self and the strategic capacity to affect today's learning for tomorrow's world. In 'Where do I fit in?' we will discuss practice that achieves educational purpose through structure while supporting people during disruption. We will reflect on a transformative approach that moves students and teachers from engagement to empowerment through relatedness, autonomy, competence and relevance in 'How can I best serve others?' Finally, you will have the opportunity to respond to the question 'Whose am I?' by thinking through how to bring your own value through the leadership that orientates to your school community.

# WHO AM I?

## Continuous learners and unlearners: The character of leaders who orientate

What, then, might it mean to be game changers who lead towards continuous learning and transformation? And how might we prepare ourselves for this role? Our leadership should begin with who we are, flow into who we want to become and be demonstrated through our actions in service of others. Confronting the inevitable gap between our leadership intentions and behaviours in our schools means reflecting on the following realities:

- We are all still learning about leadership.
- Our intentions and execution will most likely need to improve from here onwards.
- We will make mistakes along the way.

- Our leadership must be focused on doing the hard things.
- Our leadership must be focused on helping other people.
- Our leadership must help people change to become the people they need to be.
- Our leadership must be sustainable and achievable.
- Our leadership needs integrity – even though it's hard and it makes us vulnerable.
- If we are not prepared to do this, we shouldn't do the job.
- We should be prepared to do this – because we most likely can.

Our ongoing leadership as continuous learners and unlearners requires us to apply the habits of reflection further to find workable answers to these practical and profound questions:

- How do I lead my friends?
- How do I balance collaboration with control?
- How do I find the time to lead?
- How do I help others find the time to do the work of growth and transformation?
- How can I build a narrative for change that helps people to grow?
- How can I build a positive culture of constructive behaviour?
- How can I talk with other people successfully about sensitive issues or challenges?
- How can I break through with addressing destructive behaviours?
- How do I work through making decisions that can't please everyone?
- How do I manage parental expectations?
- How do I inspire students to commit to their learning and work together?

To answer these questions we need to want to contribute effectively to the growth, progress, achievement, success and qualification of others in developing their own character, competency and wellness. We will also need to work with those in our community of inquiry and practice to define and honour the terms of the new social contract for education that a school for tomorrow exists to serve: today's learning for tomorrow's world. We will need to understand that complex educational environments place difficult, challenging and contradictory demands on leaders. Long-term success in educational leadership lies in clear purpose and direction, strong values, and an organisational belief that is underpinned by individual and community-wide adaptive expertise and self-efficacy.

Professionally, leaders will need to move beyond their own immediate context – their personal needs and desires and those of their closest colleagues and friends – to gain both a little distance and a whole lot of perspective about what matters most. To orientate a school community towards the fullest expression of the civic, performance and moral character that lies at the heart of its graduate outcomes, leaders will need a deep consciousness for 'the other'. This awareness must inform an understanding that they are stewards in schools where each individual person, the young people and adults in our care, is home to a unique life. They must meet challenges, find new and better ways of doing things, accept greater levels of responsibility, recognise and embrace the implicit need to make decisions, manage risk, form judgements and act on them in a way that promotes the purpose of their schools while upholding their values and culture.

Thus, in keeping with the third graduate outcome of a school for tomorrow as continuous learners and unlearners who wish to orientate their communities towards transformation, leaders must acquire, model and encourage the character, competency and wellness that they want their students and staff to demonstrate.

### Learn

Continuous learners and unlearners prepare for a lifetime of learning, including the unlearning and relearning that will be required along their pathway to excellence. They also inspire others to grow within the context of the volume, pace and intensity of our times.

### Live

They seek to be equipped to become dynamic learners who are committed to continuing growth and improvement throughout their lives. They harness their curiosity, resourcefulness and adaptability to help us to transform gracefully from who we are today to the people we need to be in the future. They encourage others to become better at continually developing their competencies.

### Lead

They embrace change in their lives. They are aware that change readiness involves acquiring ongoing personal growth and transformation by adopting a process of adaptive expertise and self-efficacy. This relies on the capacity to take responsibility for learning from all situations with a willing, open and agile mind that can assemble and master a dynamic and volatile body of knowledge and that is informed by past practice, current experience and the anticipation of future needs.

### Work

They are grounded in learning about transformation, which helps them acquire knowledge of approaches to learning that build self-efficacy and adaptive expertise; gain skills in successful research, development and the implementation of new ideas; nurture a disposition towards action, movement and taking positive steps towards progress; and build the capacity to reflect on the relationship between their change readiness and their continuous personal growth.

## Building learning: The purpose of leaders who orientate

So what does continuous learning look like? How do we recognise transformation in a school and the lives of the members of its community? What is the purpose of game changers in this respect?

Game changers orientate their schools towards transformation through continuous learning by exercising the strategic lever of building learning capacity. They build an agreed approach to learning in their community and, as a consequence of well-developed change readiness, they produce more graduates who can learn and unlearn continuously. They consistently institute a desire to grow from experiences of the whole of learning to improve outcomes for more students. They measure and evaluate these outcomes. To do this, they routinely gather and evaluate data-based evidence of agreed school growth and transformation that relate to the core learning, leadership, character, service, sport, co-curricular and developmental activity of their school. They also do so for the financial, governance and business stewardship of the resources needed to attain the educational mission of their school. In their planning, they are deliberate, targeted and intentional.

They are driven by a relentless passion for and shared practice in setting, planning for, attaining and (where possible) improving their school's capacity to deliver outcomes for its learners. They do so by building cultures of excellence in leadership and learning, cumulative internal data-gathering, regular programs of review and external research of other available options. They define and improve their standards. They encourage the ongoing growth transformation of their school by setting robust and consistent standards, providing support, monitoring progress, recognising success and encouraging accountability.

They also create a shared understanding among the learning community about what continuous learning and transformation should look and feel like. It's not enough for schools to imagine what the physical structures and facilities that support learning will become. The key to the vision of a school for the future starts with building a picture of the nature of learning and the needs that will arise from this. They need to be confident about their school's capacity to meet the challenge of necessary change. They need to know that they have the mandate of their community to go about this process of change so that the right type of learning – the core business of any school – drives both the physical environment and the aligned activity of the community of inquiry and practice within a human-centred, technologically enriched ecosystem that is also people, place and planet conscious, and intentionally purposeful.

Once we have shaped an ecosystem to house today's learning for tomorrow's world, we need to understand how to shape the trajectories of our school's strategic intent and its operations towards this practice. The highest performing schools demonstrate a shared vision and vocabulary for their preferred future, an agreed values and value proposition for what they deliver and change, the velocity, shape and trajectory of which have all been designed and implemented to attend to the demands and pressures of their external and internal contexts. They deliver an excellent education for character, competency and wellness that is founded on future-fit graduate outcomes and the expression of these through a curriculum that allows them to shape their educational philosophies, programs and activities accordingly towards a preferred future as evidence-based communities of inquiry and practice. Ultimately, they are focused on improving outcomes for more learners by:

- providing a whole education (the deliberate, targeted and intentional centrality of character, competency and wellness in an excellent education)

- meeting expectations for a whole education (the creation of the secret sauce of high-performance that equips, empowers and enables a school learning culture characterised by increasing mastery in adaptive expertise and self-efficacy)

- achieving standards of excellence in a whole education (articulating and realising a shared understanding that the goal of learning relationships, which develop individual and collective transformation across a school community, is the pursuit of excellence).

The excellence of a great school is defined by its capacity to personalise, align and integrate character, competency and wellness into every student's personal learning journey of discovery. We judge this according to who the students are; what they know, can do and believe; and how they learn in pursuit of their graduate outcomes. School communities often convince themselves that what they are doing is excellent without really understanding what this standard means, especially in a world that has expectations for personalised learning within an outstanding ecosystem that prepares all students to thrive. Not only does this world continue to move fast and demand much. It also believes that education is the solution for many of its enduring challenges and that excellence is a standard that truly matches the inherent worth of each learner and our respect for their dignity as home to a unique life.

So, what do we mean by excellence? Excellence is found in something of the highest quality. It is seen in achievement at the highest level of performance; it is exemplary. It exceeds normal expectations of performance and meets the highest expectations of what can be achieved. Ultimately, a school with a strong culture of excellence is not merely good. It sets the standard to be followed and it is something of great virtue and worth. It is excellent.

Excellence in anything starts with vision, passion and will. The process for preparing a community to cultivate these begins with understanding the context. This means responding to historical perspectives of and contemporary provocations for excellence in learning, living, leading and working based on a vision for character, competency and wellness that promotes thriving. Excellence in defining the culture that might support this involves constructing a vision, rationale, standards, norms and narrative for achieving excellence in an education for character, competency and wellness. This is why the persuasive function of a leader who informs necessitates co-creation of vision. Finally, excellence in a school means cultivating the passion to be and become the best versions of ourselves by building alignment through aspirations for excellence, structural cohesion, cultural robustness and collaboration through inquiry and practice.

An excellent school therefore provides a wide field in which to inspire, stretch, challenge and support students to rehearse for their adulthood. It does so by offering many diverse encounters with excellence and experiences of character, competency and wellness within deliberately incremental and immersive learning. Like the medieval tales of old and the computer games students play now, the challenges must become harder and more important as the quest goes on. In this way, the experience of school is about becoming someone else. It is about letting go of the child who once was and the process of gaining adaptive expertise and self-efficacy through character apprenticeship that shows learners where their future on The Pathway to Excellence might lie.

Building excellence in strategic learning capacity begins with establishing and enhancing a culture of aspiration and performance within the community. The expectation for student achievement should be based on the belief that all children are capable of success – children should be supported to set goals and achieve them, regardless of their background or socioeconomic situation. Schools must have clear and ambitious expectations for students and teachers (ideally involving students and teachers in setting these standards) as well as systems of clear communication, review and feedback on achievement. Leaders need to help their community to set high expectations for learning, improvement, performance and outcomes. They need to be wary of the assumption that this is being done; these assumptions are too frequently revealed to be inconsistent with reality in schools of all types. They also need to pay attention to what works and what doesn't work in making these expectations real. They should attend to implementing practice that achieves results, measuring success and implementing feedback loops to obtain evidence and exemplars of success within systems that support learning and innovation.

Building strategic learning capacity also involves an interest in and willingness to participate in international trends in learning and teaching as well as committing to building teacher capacity to provide excellence. In particular, leaders need to understand their responsibility to build adaptive expertise and self-efficacy in the community they serve, particularly in their teachers, so that their own approaches to learning mirror the needs of the world around them. Holly Ransom, CEO of Emergent, puts it well.

## GAME CHANGER INSIGHT

'So, I think there is an enormous challenge on two fronts. One is preparing them with the skills for the future economy and making sure people are ready in a kind of technical capacity set. And then, it also gets to the heart of the pedagogy of how we teach and how we learn, because a big part of it is creating this mindset and this habit set around being a lifelong learner and what that means. It's about getting comfortable being uncomfortable and being able to be a beginner and try new things and have a go. Because the thing that we know about what the future looks like is that the pace of change we're experiencing now, by which we're all overwhelmed to some varying shape and degree, is the slowest pace of change we're going to face moving forward. This is the new normal and we've got to get used to it. Part of that is the actual way we've got to learn to work and think and lead and operate. And then part of that is in the rapidly changing kind of skills and kind of set-up of our economy that's going to actually allow people to find work or ply their trade craft in whatever way, shape or form.'

**Holly Ransom**

For schools to develop strategic learning capacity in this context, leaders need to orientate them away from rigid systems of learning and towards personalised systems focused on learner needs and the graduate outcomes for thriving. These systems need to be activated by flexible curriculum and innovative pedagogical practice. Stakeholders need to be drawn together by systems and operations that equip, empower and enable them rather than control, divide or hold apart.

Leaders can consolidate the mandate for change in strategic learning capacity by helping a community commit itself to the value of its education and its educators as the agents of transformation through continuous learning. The community and the society it serves must place a high value on education. Typically, this is reflected through levels of funding, attitude, community involvement and support. At the same time, quality teachers are key to the success of students and the teacher–student relationship is vital to making sure that well-intentioned statements about the value of education are borne out in the concrete actions of connected and supportive school stakeholders who value teachers, recognise the importance of their work and understand that their profession is complex.

Leaders need to attract high-quality candidates into their schools and then provide them with relevant and rigorous initial induction and training that helps to transform them into effective instructors and researchers. We need to build a flexible career structure that rewards both good teaching and the attainment of good learning outcomes. Teachers must be encouraged, supported and developed to take responsibility for their professional learning within the context of the changing nature of our world and the changes to the educational, human, technological and other systems that support it. We need to promote effective teachers and give them more responsibility for leading teaching and learning. And finally, we need to identify effective leaders early in their careers and prepare them through specific training and development to lead for change – and we need to support them through this process.

 **ENCOUNTER AND RESPOND**

What defines your character and purpose as a leader who orientates your school community towards transformation through continuous learning?

## WHERE DO I FIT IN?

### The practice of a leader who orientates

How can a leader who orientates help a learning community to be confident that its learning activity matches the needs of today's learning for tomorrow's world? Whether you are orientating a team or a whole school towards transformation through continuous learning, you will need to work with both structure and people to negotiate this process with success. We have made some suggestions about the essential elements of these practices in tables 4.1 and 4.2 as they manifest for leaders of teams and organisations respectively.

## Table 4.1: Orientating as a leader of a team

| | |
|---|---|
| **ACHIEVING EDUCATIONAL PURPOSE THROUGH STRUCTURE** | Introduces and manages desired changes in an intentional, goal-oriented and purposeful way, leading to a successful change process. |
| | Aligns team goals, norms and standard operating procedures to the stated expectation of the school's strategy and culture. |
| | Integrates the school's framework for education, graduate outcomes and change narrative into all aspects of the team's mission, planning and implementation. |
| **SUPPORTING PEOPLE DURING DISRUPTION** | Ensures that systems are designed around meeting the needs of individuals with a variety of personalised education approaches. |
| | Employs effective change-management processes and strategies to overcome resistance and maintain team cohesiveness. |

## Table 4.2: Orientating as a leader of an organisation

| | |
|---|---|
| **ACHIEVING EDUCATIONAL PURPOSE THROUGH STRUCTURE** | Improves organisational knowledge through personal research and experimentation. |
| | Contributes to the creation of change narratives and schoolwide culture and performance expectations. |
| | Supports the establishment and growth of the community of inquiry and practice connected with the framework for education and graduate outcomes. |
| **SUPPORTING PEOPLE DURING DISRUPTION** | Creates systems to enable the collection, analysis and then action based on meaningful student data about personalised learning. |
| | Encourages others to learn through action orientation, experimentation and action research by coaching team members and by building mentoring relationships. |

## Achieving educational purpose through structure

Successfully implementing desired change is a vital component of leadership. When the case for transformation is expressed through the vision of a school, the job of introducing and managing the desired change in an intentionally purposeful and goal-oriented way falls to leaders who orientate. Using aligned and supportive structures can be a real asset for this task.

Let's begin by thinking about this notion of purpose and the goals that flow from it. The ultimate objective of a planned change is to achieve success. We have already seen that, while attention to detail is important, perfection is impossible. Leaders need to use the structure provided by standards of performance to help them to show the way forward to achieve the agreed purpose of the school. They need to use them also to indicate the steps of iterative improvement that will help a team to know that they are making good progress towards achieving their purpose. Leaders who model, scaffold and coach will find that tools of delegation, supervision and feedback will help them to orient their teams towards the achievement of progressively higher standards, often employing new knowledge skills, dispositions and habits along the way. The key to a goal-setting approach is to use the structure of a journey of discovery and attainment to motivate team members to continue to learn and improve – to continue to move forward toward the realisation of the vision.

So, what process can you use to analyse the need for change and develop effective plans for change with a team or organisation? Think about the following steps to guide your thinking about what you can do to analyse and act on change in your school:

1. Diagnose the situation.
2. Clarify the present state.
3. Visualise the end state.
4. Predict the likely effects.
5. Answer any concerns and discuss emotional awareness.
6. Develop the plan.
7. Communicate the change.
8. Implement the plan.
9. Consolidate and follow up.

As a school's change journey proceeds, leaders should also target specific areas of the learning ecosystem as likely places where change will need to occur, bearing in mind that they are all interrelated so introducing change to one will likely have an impact on the others. These areas of leadership impact and the corresponding effects they may have on the learning ecosystem are detailed in table 4.3.

**Table 4.3: Orientating leadership impact to the learning ecosystem**

| LEADERSHIP IMPACT | | ECOSYSTEM EFFECT | |
|---|---|---|---|
| PERSONNEL AND THEIR CAPABILITIES | How leaders engage with people and their individual strengths to overcome any challenges or barriers to implementing successful change | HUMAN CENTRED | The learning context retains its focus on how all individuals can grow in character, competency and wellness to thrive in their world |
| SOFTWARE AND HARDWARE | How a change in requirement can be assisted by a change in systems, equipment or other resources | TECHNOLOGY ENRICHED | Schools use digital and technological solutions that augment and dignify human potential |
| CHANGE PROCESSES | The methods through which leaders can design and implement courses of action that contribute to positive holistic change | PEOPLE, PLACE AND PLANET CONSCIOUS | All systems and operations are conceived of in terms of their capacity to promote sustainable long-term interactions |
| FORMATION OF NORMS AND CULTURE | The way teams and their practices are shaped around the creation of aligned vision, ethos and sense of purpose | INTENTIONALLY PURPOSEFUL | The default position of the community is towards deliberate action that increases momentum towards a preferred vision |

Another way of looking at the role of structure in bringing about desired change is to consider the levels of challenge associated with that desired change – what needs to be changed and over what length of time:

1. Changing knowledge

This is the simplest process. It involves the shortest time frame and can often be achieved with minimal contact or conflict with others.

2. Changing attitudes

This is a more challenging process. It usually involves a longer time frame as people learn to change their state of mind and resulting dispositions in the face of new knowledge.

3. Changing individual behaviour

Changing the behaviours associated with new attitudes and new knowledge is an even more challenging process. It requires a longer time frame as individuals gain adaptive expertise and self-efficacy in the skills and capabilities associated with success in a new enterprise.

4. Changing team behaviour

This is the most challenging process because you must coordinate a group of people and their individual behaviours. It requires the longest time frame as you seek to create a culture in which a group can positively influence the growth of individuals in their character, competency and wellness.

It can be tempting for a leader to dwell on the first kind of change by seeking to accumulate more and more knowledge, usually in an attempt to be prepared for every possible contingency; however, unless the leader and team push through to change attitudes, individual behaviour and team behaviour, the change that is required is unlikely to be properly embedded. It is also important to understand that you will need to use a range of skills and techniques to address these different levels of change.

## Supporting people during disruption

Even desired change can be a major source of disruption for individuals and teams. With respect to this, your leadership practice should begin with an examination of yourself. Effective change leaders are themselves comfortable with ambiguity and uncertainty. They have a balance of technical and interpersonal skills. They are also capable of being tough decision-makers who are focused on performance while also being compassionate guides of their teams and nurturers of their team members. They use a range of different approaches and styles, testing each for its impact in its context and moving quickly from one to another when it is clear that the context indicates its unsuitability for the people and purpose at hand.

Even well-planned changes are difficult until the critical mass of a team adapts to the new state. Dispensing with proven ways of doing things should not be done lightly. People will already be skilled in key areas and to change their expectations and roles can and will cause them stress and uncertainty as they adapt to new situations and methods. When you introduce change you will find that your main tasks are to overcome resistance, manage team relationships and individual concerns, and maintain team cohesiveness through transition.

Transition refers to the process through which people experience change. People can find transition unsettling and can express this in unpredictable ways. Many responses are emotional. Resistance to transition can manifest in uncertainty, threatened self-interest, feelings of personal loss or relevance and conflicting perceptions. When not handled well or ignored, transition can lead to an initial reduction of productivity, morale and team commitment, regardless of whether team members want to change. Transition misalignment – when team members cannot recognise and accept the need for change – causes much of the resistance you will experience, some of which will be directed towards you through no fault of your own. Transition misalignment can be countered by communicating the intent and rationale for every change.

Leaders must be careful not to alienate team members by dumping criticism on old methods; it is better to talk about the need to adapt to new situations while acknowledging that older methods may have served the team well in the past. Most institutions view change warily; many never adapt properly. Even the most successful teams tend to take on change slowly and incrementally, introducing it gently and building it into their existing structures. It is less common for a leader to propose and then see radical change through to its conclusion, but when it does happen, it is very exciting to be part of!

As a leader you will often need to help a team to unfreeze and evaluate their current state so they can then work to lessen resistance and move into uncharted waters. This will inevitably involve overcoming internal doubts and fears. Constructive and non-judgemental dialogue about emotions and feelings, celebration of small wins and justification of the process and outcomes according to the culture of 'the way we do things here' and the values of 'what we think is the right thing to do' are all useful approaches. This can help people to see their way through to alternatives that will eventually become more palatable, despite the discomfort of change, than the status quo.

You may also need to help team members to construct a personal narrative of how they are managing their own learning in a time of change. Tracey Breese comments on the notion of a continuous learning construct for adults in this respect.

## GAME CHANGER INSIGHT

*'Be comfortable in the uncomfortable, because that's where the good learning happens. So, if you are truly a lifelong learner – which you're supposed to be as a teacher, it should be why you came into teaching – you will be comfortable in the uncomfortable, and you will be happy to fly the plane with me as we build it.'*

**Tracey Breese**

In addition to supporting their own personal learning processes, you will need to educate team members about the broader context of the change process and help them manage their own emotional responses to it. You should be prepared to justify and re-justify the need for change and endow all levels within your team with ownership of that change. Other strategies for overcoming resistance to change in the team include setting new challenges, promoting participation in and contribution to the possible solutions and eventual decisions, and providing appropriate rewards. You will most likely need to use a combination of facilitation, support, negotiation and compromise to reach achievement, although you will need to be careful not to water down your standards or expectations for achievement. It is better to propose a more gradual timescale for attaining goals than it is to lighten the load altogether. Teams thrive when they rise to a challenge and demonstrate to themselves that they can manage their fears and grow together as they experience the adversity of disruption.

Successful change processes often begin with the sharing of a vision and the creation of a plan for change that both promote acceptance of the need (and often compulsion) to change. These processes are enhanced by building individual and team capacity both in the competencies needed for the change and in the disposition towards change itself, and achieving initial and ongoing milestones that speak to the articulation and reinforcement of the rationale for the new state of play.

###  ENCOUNTER AND RESPOND

How might you measure the nature and success of your change-management practice in your school as a leader who orientates both your teams and the organisations you serve?

# HOW CAN I BEST SERVE OTHERS?

## Transformation: The approach of leaders who orientate

So, what will motivate members of a school community to engage in transformation so that, in time, we might empower them to become transformed? As leaders who orientate, our starting point should be the inherent psychological needs that are the basis for an individual's human motivation, personality development and the self-regulation of their behaviour. To do so we need to differentiate between autonomous (intrinsic) motivation and controlled (extrinsic) motivation. When individuals are driven by intrinsic motivation they feel self-directed and autonomous; when they are driven by extrinsic motivation they can feel pressured to behave in a certain way without the feeling of autonomy. In the context of how we learn, live, lead and work at school, intrinsic motivation is bound up in and influenced by a set of beliefs and self-perceptions that individual learners develop in how they learn, live, lead and work. These include attitude and awareness, self-concept, interest, relevance and curiosity, self-efficacy, value, and setting and reaching goals.

Some extrinsic motivation can be helpful to develop initial momentum or to get us back on track when we falter or pause. But if learners – both students and staff – aren't empowered by the deep inner drive of intrinsic motivation, they won't invest in the process needed to build the required competency, attain mastery and ultimately apply this to how they learn, live, lead and work. They won't thrive.

As leaders we can have a profound influence on how we orientate learners towards the intrinsic motivation and the accompanying profoundness that is born from purpose. We can help to move them from engagement to empowerment. Cameron Fox, founding head of VERSO International School in Bangkok, Thailand, confirms this important investment in moving from the comfort expectation of engagement to the personal agency and intrinsic motivation of empowerment.

### GAME CHANGER INSIGHT

*'I think that's the investment, the investment in that belief that if you continuously think and encourage kids and adults to stay agile, not to seek the comfort of predictability, but life as an exciting space, and we should be thriving in that space, I think that's a powerful sort of coordinate for people to use.'*

Cameron Fox

Harnessing the power of intrinsic motivation through connection can be thoroughly satisfying and much more effective in the long term. Once learners become motivated to achieve, they will eventually exert their effort, time and energy in applying their knowledge, skills, dispositions and habits to become better versions of themselves. They will be growing in character, competency and wellness, then using these to solve known and new problems. This is adaptive expertise. They will be organising themselves and how they learn, live, lead and work to optimise their character, competency and wellness so that they can thrive in their world. This is self-efficacy. Eventually, they will begin to self-actualise because they can self-determine. This is the core of transformational learning.

There are four specific types of connection that teachers can use to help their learners to experience this in a continuous learning model:

1. Relatedness

What are you doing to connect yourself to those whom you lead? People are more motivated to achieve when they have formed the belief that their leader deeply cares about them as a person and their growth. Building this level of trust involves sharing who you are and learning who your students are. You can begin by building an inclusive community in your space, where the dignity of each person is valued and accepted. Humour, storytelling, positivity and passion can make all the difference in establishing a positive environment where everyone can learn. Establishing a designed relationship of character apprenticeship provides people with a sense of stability, safety and belonging and this can set the stage for more risk-taking in a respectful climate. You need to provide quality one-on-one formative feedback, encourage open and active participation and always see the good (as well as the challenges) in your people.

2. Autonomy

What are you doing to connect your people to a real sense of their voice, agency and advocacy? When we shift the focus of a culture of a team or community to its impact on the capacity of individuals to take responsibility for their own achievement through self-determination, we connect to their interests, needs and personal goals. We can create experiences that ignite curiosity, develop their passion and potentially unleash creativity. Controlling a task too much will lead, at best, to a state of compliance. People will be more motivated and perform better when they feel as though they have autonomy, control over their learning and choice in how they curate and demonstrate their competencies: knowledge, skills, dispositions and learning habits. This type of agency comes from the power to act and requires all individuals to have the ability to make decisions about their actions throughout the entire process. Providing choice can be messy. People completing different tasks at different rates can make it hard to be consistent with tracking and monitoring progress. However, once you give people more ownership for how they learn, live, lead and work, you will help them to become more self-directed and empowered. This is how we secure better outcomes for more people.

3. Competence

What are you doing to connect your people to a growth mindset? Individuals are more motivated to persist at a challenging task when they honestly believe they can grow and emerge better than they were before they began it, particularly when they have experienced success in overcoming adversity in stages. This requires them (and us!) to cultivate a growth mindset (Dweck, 2006): the belief that intelligence and ability can evolve through deliberate practice and sustained effort. Creating an environment where all learners are encouraged to take risks in pursuit of learning and growth rather than perfection is absolutely foundational to shifting to an intrinsic motivation and empowerment mindset. You need to begin the task from where individuals are right now and not worry about what came before. The task needs to be within their zone of proximal development and allow for a natural productive struggle that stretches and challenges for growth to emerge and for the individual to ultimately thrive. Remember that growth needs do not stem from a lack of something, but rather from a natural desire to grow as a person by enhancing a sense of belonging, the capacity to fulfil one's own potential and the capacity to do what is good and right in life. Growth and character development go hand in hand.

4. Relevance

What are you doing to connect the intended process of learning to how your people need to learn, live, lead and work? Individuals are less motivated to undertake complex tasks that require creativity, adaptability and perseverance by extrinsic rewards and more by the inherent value of growth and development when these are made relevant to their lives. When individuals believe they are doing something authentic, something that will improve their professional capacity or have some kind of tangible impact that they value, they are naturally motivated to engage and (therefore) ready for empowerment. If you only focus on short-term, extrinsic rewards to coax people through low-level tasks instead of designing authentic and personal experiences that draw on each person's natural curiosity, passion and interests, you will not truly connect and empower each and all in your team or community. Experiences in which each individual and team gets to solve a challenge that is meaningful and relevant to their context can empower all to act and do something that matters to them and for others.

> ## ⏸ ENCOUNTER AND RESPOND
>
> We invite you to encounter and respond to a process of thinking differently about empowering leadership:
>
> - What does empowering through relatedness, autonomy, competence and relevance as a leader look like in your school? What *should* it look like in your school?
> - What could it mean to think differently about leading through empowerment in your context? What kinds of changes can you make to your leadership practice to support this?

## WHOSE AM I?

As leaders who orientate our schools towards transformation through continuous learning, we're changing the game of education right now. What are the rules of the game? The continuous learning that is relevant to our times is not the same as learning in a traditional school environment – we need a new model. The model that is being created right now draws on the wisdom, adaptive expertise and self-efficacy of colleagues all over the world who might never have imagined it possible to do what they are. We can make this new model real – and we are. We are realising that less is more, that our values and relationships are essential for supporting learning and that the physical, personal and emotional needs of our students cannot be overlooked by systems. We are holding on to the essential and enduring components of education, even if we are finding new ways they might be manifested.

Creating successful learning that goes way beyond our previous experiences of school is both possible and desirable. We can't imagine that we will go back to exactly what we had before, unchanged by the evidence of what is working now in the new world environment. The exact possibilities of this new model are not yet clear and it is necessary to experiment and iterate in an environment where less is more and connection requires collaboration, voice and agency from all. Our humanity is at the heart of what we are doing, so we need to take good care of it individually and together.

> ## (II) ENCOUNTER AND RESPOND
>
> Are you a leader who orientates? We invite you to encounter the following reflective questions and respond to them by identifying two to three priorities for your own professional learning and the growth of your adaptive expertise and self-efficacy as a leader who orientates:
>
> - How do I employ effective change-management processes and strategies to overcome resistance and maintain team cohesiveness?
>
> - How do I introduce and manage desired changes in an intentional, goal-oriented and purposeful way, leading to a successful change process?
>
> - How do I encourage creative thinking in my organisation using concepts like brainstorming, parallel thinking, lateral thinking and devil's advocate?
>
> - How do I improve organisational knowledge through my consistent contributions of personal research and experimentation?
>
> - How do I align my team's goals, norms and standard operating procedures to the meaningful stated expectations of my school's strategy and culture?

As leaders who orientate, we need to attune our teams and organisations towards the normal and necessary change that carries us forward to a preferred future. We need to help our team members to become future ready and future fit in every respect. We need to cultivate and maintain a personal and shared commitment towards the growth that is needed to acquire the character, competency and wellness that we all need to thrive in a new world environment. In the next chapter we will think through how, in the first instance, we can focus current momentum towards transformation through continuous learning and achieve better outcomes for more learners by concentrating on performance in the fundamentals of a good school.

# CHAPTER 5
# Leadership that focuses

## CREATING THE FUNDAMENTALS OF A GOOD SCHOOL: INTRODUCING LEADERSHIP THAT FOCUSES

It should be clear by now that, as school leaders, we need to focus on what lies ahead for our learners and their transformation. We need to think about the essential character and related competencies of knowledge, skills, dispositions and learning habits. These are all both timeless and pragmatically contemporary in their relevance to a world where social building blocks, such as family, identity, gender, work, employment, recreation and nationality, are shifting into new and unclear formats.

Throughout the world, expectations of schools have typically taken into account some notion of the development of character, competency and wellness outcomes – namely, the understanding that through the experiences of school, students will absorb the core values and personal attributes at the heart of that school's mission. While some may feel that the fundamentals of a good school are enduring (and to a certain extent we would agree on the 'what' of today's learning for tomorrow's world), there are signs that the expectations of stakeholder groups in schools all over the world changing dramatically and even insistently over time in nuance, emphasis and articulation (the 'how' and the 'why'). Evidence from our global research suggests that many schools are moving beyond that traditional understanding (while steadfastly preserving that heritage and tradition at its most durable and honourable).

When directly questioned about what they want for their children, very few stakeholders in these schools point specifically to only one field of achievement as the desirable goal (though some may refer to specific academic and sporting results as part of incidental conversation). The language of today's stakeholders is increasingly expressed in terms of the development of 'the whole person' and, by extension, the development of the character and competencies that comprise this. Their mandate can be summarised as follows: 'Know us, know our children, respond accordingly in your practice and show us how they are growing as whole people who can thrive in the new world environment.'

Many stakeholders, in evaluating their schools' capacities against relevant performance standards, understand the challenge of defining the fundamentals of a whole education and locating those fundamentals down the essential corridors of a school: culture, leadership, learning, performance, strategy, and systems and operations – the topics for the standards that we will examine later in this chapter as well as the six core areas of the leadership capabilities of this book. Moving a school's performance in these six fundamentals to a standard that might be recognised across our industry as 'good' seems to be about the quality, consistency and attention to detail in meeting expectations for delivering an education for the whole person. Schools that build good performance can ensure they meet these expectations in the eyes of their stakeholders because they understand – as Eric Sheninger, former teacher and principal, and now associate partner at the International Center for Leadership in Education, argues – how to ask and answer the right questions about the fundamentals of today's learning for tomorrow's world.

> **GAME CHANGER INSIGHT**
>
> 'What do our learners need for success now and in the future? The world of work has changed. Kids need to be able to self-regulate. They need to be experts in remote collaboration. They need to be able to think critically and solve complex problems that are connected to real world scenarios. They need to exhibit emotional intelligence. They need to be able to manage their time, and they have to be creative thinkers and doers ... When we look at the learning environment, is it personalised? Is it equitable? Would you want to learn under the same conditions as your kids? ... Is our teaching helping kids learn? ... Are we collecting good data? And are we using that data to put the kids on a different trajectory? ... And it all comes out of relationships – without trust, there's no relationship. If there's no relationship, no real learning occurs. What's real learning? It's relevant. It's engaging. It's authentic. It's lasting.'
>
> Eric Sheninger

So, the leadership that focuses does so because it looks beyond the game of school itself while ensuring that the fundamentals are in place. It concentrates its school's focus on solutions for its students' future, derived from the best possible thinking. This is characterised by enacting strategic intent, operationalising this through careful and iterative implementation, and emphasising the achievement of desired graduate outcomes demonstrating character, competency and wellness. Leaders who focus draw on the leadership capability of problem-solving and decision-making, particularly through the exercise of their own adaptive expertise and self-efficacy.

In this chapter we look at the leadership competency of focusing and how leaders can focus the members and teams of their school communities on creating a good standard of performance across the fundamentals of a future-fit education. In 'Who am I?' we will explore the character and purpose of solution architects who build performance directed towards both students and improvement. In 'Where do I fit in?' we will discuss problem-solving and decision-making practice that is both well-considered and imaginative. We will reflect on the intentional approach that creates both shared purpose and a living history for a school in 'How can I best serve others?' Finally, you will have the opportunity to respond to the question 'Whose am I?' by thinking through how you bring your own value to your school community with the leadership that focuses.

# WHO AM I?

## Solution architects: The character of leaders who focus

Schools and their leaders can't stand still. They need to contemplate what it is that students will need in a world where most of the jobs of the future have not yet been invented. We have formed the view that schools should adopt three trajectories in their strategic educational development work to help them think through the focus for their performance. These trajectories can be articulated by the following positive statements:

- Good schools examine character, competency and wellness in depth.

These schools place character, competency and wellness at the core of the work of education. This is seen as the essential preparation for students to thrive in the new world context, not as an additional thing to be done. Effective solutions in this area are not pre-packaged but rather focus on solutions that both build on the work of others and take into account a school's unique context. To be a good school, they need to develop an evidence-based approach to describing and implementing a framework for an education for character, competency and wellness and an ongoing conversation within their communities about how best to ensure a world-class approach.

- Good schools are thorough about educating their students for character, competency and wellness.

A strategic and intentional approach towards an education for character, competency and wellness is more successful than reliance on assumptions about what might be happening in classrooms and other learning environments. The accidental and incidental 'caught, not taught' approach fails to provide high-quality education for character, competency and wellness to all students. A good school will want to work towards systematic formal and informal means of character education for each student, implementing a range of both proven and innovative collective, collaborative and personalised strategies that are regularly evaluated for their quality and effectiveness.

- Good schools measure what they do.

This is based on the belief that character, competency and wellness can be described and that changes in student outcomes in these areas can be both tracked and measured in a variety of qualitative and quantitative ways. The impact of an education for character, competency and wellness can also be measured, allowing a school to know where there is good value in exerting its efforts and resources. A good school should develop systems that help it to replace assertion based on anecdote with knowledge based on evidence in the discourse of every member of the community, especially when it comes to a whole education for character, competency and wellness. As we go about the work of creating a good school, therefore, we need to gather data progressively and conduct appropriate analysis of results across all of the competencies of learn, live, lead and work. We also need to appropriately measure character development and levels of wellness. Evaluation of this data should take place in alignment with the values, principles, mission and graduate outcomes that comprise a school's ethos and define its values proposition. This must also be evaluated in alignment with the goals set by that school to measure the achievement of its value proposition. At the same time, schools should implement evaluation processes to demonstrate the development of a supportive school climate that actively encourages holistic student achievement. Our global research tells us that for schools to create and sustain the right climate and environment for the secret sauce for high-performance (detailed in Chapter 6), they must make deft judgements about the placement of evaluation systems and processes. They must also determine the right measures to prioritise the right type of holistic student achievement within the warp and weft of school life.

With this in mind, let's consider the character of solution architects, the fourth graduate outcome of a school for tomorrow that leaders who want to be game changers need to model for their communities.

## Learn

Solution architects aim to design and generate effective solutions to emerging problems and issues. Inspired by the intention of sustainability, they are equipped to provide direction supported by answers to the questions of a world that seeks clarity and certainty in circumstances that are rapidly evolving and multidimensional.

## Live

They are motivated to become committed coaches who think carefully to generate practical and workable answers to challenging questions. They use grit, perseverance and attention to detail to give others the confidence to meet expectations by thinking through options and constructing, testing, implementing and evaluating solutions to familiar and unfamiliar problems. They chart a course toward a better normal and a shared understanding of excellence.

### Lead

They think through problems with confidence. They know that creative and critical thinking competency involves eliciting direction by asking significant questions and developing solutions that meet expectations. This relies on the capacity to use conventional and innovative processes of reflection to analyse alternative arguments, evaluate evidence and create content.

### Work

They are grounded in learning about sustainable expectations, which helps them to acquire knowledge of tangible models for achieving desirable process and product outcomes; gain skills in considering and evaluating a range of possible options; nurture a disposition towards using both evidence and judgement to assess the impact of solutions; and build the capacity to reflect on the success of their critical and creative thinking in giving appropriate direction. Not every solution will be new, but all solutions will be crafted from an abiding curiosity about the world and an inclination to simply try new things. Solution architects never want to stand still and accept the status quo as the inevitable model or process of doing things.

The starting point in schools for leadership that focuses is a focus on students. It sounds so simple – a mantra that many of us recite weekly, if not daily. While sports, music, drama, debating, reading programs, pastoral care, wellbeing systems and so much of what is traditionally associated with and promoted by schools are important as ways to support an education for good character, our message is that a future-focused character education is not about these things, per se. They may be part of the future for our students – or they may not. At the end of the day, practices such as these must be tested against the rationale that they are supposed to serve, not retain an untouchable status without examination. Some of our existing honourable traditions may be part of the solutions that we co-create. If they do what they're supposed to, they will be fine. If not, then they should go the way of any number of previously time-honoured practices that we no longer carry out because they are no longer fit for purpose. Ultimately, if we think that the unthinking habituation of specific received rituals and practices that we ourselves like is the way we build the adults of tomorrow, we need to think again.

The thinking about corridors of experience and opportunity that should exist in a school to lead to pathways to success has been consolidated into what we have articulated as the six graduate outcomes of a school for tomorrow. This refers, of course, to the corridors that guide the experience of the whole of learning for students (including the processes and supportive ecosystem that support this experience) and encourage them to apply their character, competency and wellness to experience success in a world that needs them to:

- have the integrity to lead meaningful lives as good people
- have the ability to manage complexity with authenticity as future builders
- grow and transform themselves as continuous learners and unlearners
- provide sustainable direction to the world as solution architects
- balance the local, the regional and the global with perspective as responsible citizens
- work well in relationship with others to bring success and fulfillment for all of us as team creators.

As the context of the world moves towards the reality of an interconnected technology-rich community, we know already that the expectations for the outcomes that students might achieve are not what they once were. As we have suggested throughout this book, there is now a shared expectation across schools and systems that all students will graduate with the capacity to thrive in their world. Families demand the best possible education for their children. They want this to unlock a lifetime of possibilities and to create pathways to success for them.

## Building performance: The purpose of leaders who focus

We know that our schools need to strive to help children be thoroughly equipped for entry into the adult world. And yet, as with all human institutions, no school is perfect. Some schools will excel in many areas, while others have a more limited range of excellence. Some communities are very involved in their support of their teachers and their schools; in other schools the work of the staff is enhanced by only the core of the community. What is common to all schools, regardless of the level of families' involvement in the day-to-day work, is their capacity to improve what it is that they do. The expectations of today may be challenging enough for many in education. Yet our world keeps demanding that we reappraise what these expectations might be and how we might deliver on them.

So, how can schools best approach this task of improving performance? A disposition towards and willingness to identify improvement originates in the values of a school and is cultivated through the relationships of people within that school's community. This needs to be matched by a willingness to ask difficult and constructive questions. As observed by Greg Miller, asking these difficult questions must become part of what we do.

> ## GAME CHANGER INSIGHT
>
> *'We have to ask ourselves: How is the action taking place in this learning space at this very time contributing towards our vision? ... It's about questioning everything. We question everything. It doesn't mean we have stopped doing everything associated with the old paradigm, because there is research around good practice such as didactic teaching and the teacher at the front of the room that still plays a part of the work we do because it has to. So, very clear instructional learning, led by a teacher, is a part of what we do, but it's not the only thing that we do ... This requires (sometimes behind closed doors) fairly direct conversations that will see teachers question us as to whether what we're doing is honouring our intent that student choice, voice and agency is central to all that we do.'*
>
> Greg Miller

The belief in student voice and agency that Miller refers to in this insight is important. Schools need to believe that, in keeping with their ethos and purpose, they can achieve the best possible outcomes for all of their students. They need to welcome the capacity to change what they do so that they can more effectively achieve better performance across all of the fundamentals of what makes schools good. They need to stretch beyond that to contemplate the excellence that high-performance culture can bring, although they should be realistic about the journey towards exhibiting this across every aspect of school life. As we have seen already, excellence is a rare commodity – although the pursuit of it should characterise all strategy and operations in the life of a school.

We advocate for backwards mapping (known also as *backwards planning*) from context from values to purpose to graduate outcomes to strategy to practice. In other words, what we do must flow from why we want to do it. The dog wags the tail; it's not the tail wagging the dog. It is clear to us from our work that unless we align what we do to our mission, values, ethos, strategy, implementation and outcomes – unless we have the integrity of good culture that reflects its purpose – we run the risk that the arcane or even eccentric ephemera on the periphery of our practice will end up defining what we do in educating for character, not the principles and purpose at the centre.

Let's have a look at what these fundamentals of performance might be, drawing on the six global standards derived from CIRCLE's ongoing research program.

## Table 5.1: Six global standards of thriving

| | |
|---|---|
| **BUILDING CULTURE** | Supports the whole work of a school that develops the civic, performance and moral character of its learners in a deliberate way so that they might become good people of integrity who know the way, go the way and show the way forward on The Pathway to Excellence. |
| **BUILDING LEADERSHIP** | Supports the construction of a compelling narrative about the progress of a school from yesterday to today to tomorrow that prepares future builders to help others to interpret and navigate through complexity, particularly through their capacity to communicate. |
| **BUILDING LEARNING** | Supports the ongoing learning journey of a school that develops the adaptive expertise and self-efficacy of continuous learners and unlearners to grow in character, competency and wellness, achieve success in the school's graduate outcomes, and thrive in their world. |
| **BUILDING PERFORMANCE** | Supports the establishment and maintenance of a culture of high-performance in which solution architects learn how to ask the right questions to produce evidence-based and research-driven answers to multidimensional problems. |
| **BUILDING STRATEGY** | Using future-fit thinking to create and implement a strategy that will ensure the attainment of the school's preferred future by encouraging the responsible citizenship of learners with the perspective to balance the needs of their local, regional and global communities. |
| **BUILDING SYSTEMS AND OPERATIONS** | Refining the knowledge engine of a school so that it becomes a community of inquiry and practice focused on improved outcomes for learners who collaborate with each other as team creators. |

While it may seem obvious, sharpening the focus of your community on seeking improvement across standards such as these is a first-order task for you as a leader with the responsibility to achieve the desired outcomes for your school. The cultural change required to effect this can take some thought about how best to influence the different groups involved. One piece of advice that we can offer is that the greatest support for change can be the energy and enthusiasm of your students, so long as this amplifies their sense of voice, agency and advocacy. At the same time, their natural inexperience and either caution or excitement at the prospect of change will create a need for careful and sensitive mentoring by adults and other students.

Your use of the strategic lever of building performance will encourage your school to produce graduates who become solution architects who display creative and critical thinking, and to recognise and work towards high performance. Throughout the school you will help people to appreciate the importance of evidence-based practice to develop solutions for building cultures of excellence in a whole education. As they do so, they will increasingly believe in their capacity to solve problems and meet the expectations of their community in a structured fashion. You need to assert confidence in the capacity of all to be successful and privilege the disciplined pursuit of achievement by encouraging the attainment of individual and collective goals that challenge every member of your community to move beyond where they are now and towards what they might become in the future.

You also need to be committed to identifying the broad and deep nature of stakeholder satisfaction within your school community by testing the validity of assumptions and anecdotes against key data about performance in key academic, pastoral and business outcomes. You will help others to achieve tangible outcomes for students and programs that meet expectations. Finally, and most importantly, in routinely thinking first of students you will establish and achieve process and product goals for students and programs that are appropriate to both the context of the learning environment and the deliberate and targeted focus of learning. This focus is particularly relevant in the areas of student care and character, learning culture across the curriculum and co-curriculum, and the design and delivery of student programs and pathways characterised by how they promote student voice, leadership, diversity, innovation and future-readiness.

## ⊚ ENCOUNTER AND RESPOND

What defines your character and purpose as a leader who focuses your school community towards transformation through the model of a solution architect?

# WHERE DO I FIT IN?

## The practice of a leader who focuses

Problem-solving and decision-making are central to the practice of leaders who focus. What characterises any leader is that they must make decisions about what to do or not do in any given circumstance and take responsibility for those decisions. There will almost always be choices available, but a leader must be able to say, in the words of United States President Harry S Truman, 'The buck stops here!' From what we have seen in the work of successful leaders in schools around the world, effective decision-making practice is about your capacity to make timely decisions that engage your team and fulfil your purpose while managing the stress and risk associated with those decisions. Tables 5.2 and 5.3 describe this problem-solving and decision-making leadership practice at team and organisational levels.

### Table 5.2: Focusing as a leader of a team

| PROBLEM-SOLVING AND DECISION-MAKING | Employs a range of appropriate problem-solving and decision-making models that result in timely personal decisions to meet the desired objective. |
| --- | --- |
| | Employs team members appropriately in making decisions and avoids poor thinking in the process. |
| | Successfully manages the stress and risk associated with making decisions. |

### Table 5.3: Focusing as a leader of an organisation

| PROBLEM-SOLVING AND DECISION-MAKING | Measures and analyses critical data that make a difference in achieving team goals. |
| --- | --- |
| | Makes timely decisions on behalf of the team and takes appropriate action on these decisions |
| | Puts concepts and plans into action and achieves goals |

## Create choices, make decisions and solve problems

The basis of the success for much of the problem-solving and decision-making that you do as a leader will come down to your willingness to focus on preparing for what lies ahead. At the heart of this will be your attention to detail. You must become good at demonstrating basic skills and absorbing the knowledge needed to lead by example. You need to be prepared to show your team how to do what it needs to do and what it needs to know. You cannot expect to deal with difficult challenges until you know how to do enough of the simple things required for your decisions to be carried out, and you cannot attempt to grapple with complex ideas until you have mastery over the basic details that inform the circumstances surrounding your decisions.

A simple model for decision-making is to define the problem, identify the objective of the decision, analyse the situation, identify and assess the alternative, decide the best course of action, implement the plan and evaluate the results. Beware adopting your immediate favourite or the first course of action that occurs to you without considering alternatives. Use balanced, critical judgement and be willing to evaluate the options before choosing the course of action that seems to best meet the needs of the people, place and planet. To do so you will need to think through the positive and negative consequences of potential choices objectively and consider the impact they will have on those involved. Making judgements on this basis will require you to gather information and process the facts and details at hand, taking into account your intuition about how best to analyse and interpret this data.

Sometimes it is the quality of the questions we ask and our capacity to focus them on the heart of the issues that matter the most that can help us reach decisions that are more likely to work. From our global research practice at a School for tomorrow. we have derived a set of ten observations and associated questions about the practice of today's learning for tomorrow's world. Leaders can refer to these questions, set out in table 5.4, when thinking about the preferred future of their learning community and the ecosystem that they will want to construct for it.

## Table 5.4: Practising and leading today's learning for tomorrow's world

| THE PRACTICE OF TODAY'S LEARNING FOR TOMORROW'S WORLD | THE PROVOCATION OF THE GAME CHANGER WHOSE LEADERSHIP FOCUSES ON TRANSFORMATION THROUGH CONTINUOUS LEARNING |
| --- | --- |
| The values set for education draws on tradition and is sharpened by our contemporary circumstances. | How will our school balance the needs of yesterday, today and tomorrow? |
| All aspects of schooling need to be both aligned and personalised. | How can our school bring about the institutional focus and discipline needed to make today's learning for tomorrow's world a reality? |
| The leading schools of the world have a clear vision for learning informed by graduate outcomes that speak to the character, competency and wellness required to thrive in the new world environment. | How will our school demonstrate the pervasive and constructive influence of a graduate profile on all of the educational activity of our school? |
| Educational research across the world points to teacher performance as the key to achieving graduate outcomes. | How will our school ensure that data collection, systems, structures and resources encourage the best possible performance of our staff? |
| The best teaching works to improve outcomes for learners within a learning culture that is enriched by reflection and inquiry. | How will our school help its community understand the primacy of students asking and answering the right questions to understand and improve their own performance? |
| The disposition and habits of the best teachers are based on adaptive expertise and self-efficacy. | What can our school do to enhance the mastery, autonomy and purpose of its teachers so that they are committed to outstanding outcomes for themselves, their team, their school and, most importantly, their students? |

Continued...

| THE PRACTICE OF TODAY'S LEARNING FOR TOMORROW'S WORLD | THE PROVOCATION OF THE GAME CHANGER WHOSE LEADERSHIP FOCUSES ON TRANSFORMATION THROUGH CONTINUOUS LEARNING |
|---|---|
| We can help teachers to become better with an effective coaching and goal-setting process. | How will our school help its teachers to welcome their involvement in performance development? |
| Teaching operates in a technologically rich society that is open and informed by data at all levels. | How can you encourage your school to become more technologically savvy and more transparent in its approach to generating and sharing data with stakeholders? |
| The ongoing pattern of change and renewal that we see in schools needs to be predictive of rather than responsive to what we see in society. | How can you help your school to build a culture of research and development that helps you to construct the best solutions for your future? |
| Educational leadership works best when it attends to deliberate, targeted and intentional strategy that builds the right culture for a learning community that leads its society. | How can you encourage your school to design its preferred future? |

Often leaders use their teams to help them make decisions. Group thinking promotes high cohesion and group commitment, employs a greater range of knowledge and experience, and uses group synergy, where team members stimulate new ideas and solutions through mutual encouragement, creativity, innovation and influence. On the other hand, it can lead to pressure to conform, result in domination by one group member or clique, extend the time taken to reach a decision or encourage groupthink, where the desire for consensus overcomes realism and moral judgement. Thus, you will need to trust others and understand their point of view but also have the courage to rely on your own capacity to make significant, far-reaching and ethical decisions, then lead by example in carrying them out.

It is important that you complement this willingness to involve your team in generating solutions with the willingness to be honest and demanding in your evaluation of performance – your performance, your team's performance and the performance of individual members. A good leader is not afraid to identify the little things that need fixing and insist on them being fixed. If performance is not high enough yet, a little gentle and constructive criticism can go a long way in helping your team to understand that, while you value them, you need to raise the standard together.

Great leaders can even be a little prophetic in character. They tend to critique the apparent forces of conformity that render people numb. They energise people to an alternative way of seeing and living in this world. They seem to be wise to the ways in which the experience of a problem unfolds and they are adventurous, ambitious, creative and flexible in their problem-solving. They seem to anticipate the challenges that lie ahead and help their teams to develop innovative and effective solutions, then rehearse what they need to do to meet the challenges by practising their skills and applying their knowledge. Valerie Hannon understands this aspiration of problem-solving agents of change.

> **GAME CHANGER INSIGHT**
>
> 'I believe and I hope that young people can be the change-makers they need to be to shape the world. Not just the external world, but their internal worlds as well. The world, what they experience internally, they need to be shaping that. And to do so, they need to be agents of change and to experience a sense of their own possibility and power. And that's what we've all got to work for.'
>
> **Valerie Hannon**

At the same time, great leaders focus their team members' responses to challenging situations on the propensity to experiment through curiosity and wonder. They nurture our imagination and creativity, showing us that playing around with possibility enables us to put together ideas and information in ways that may not have been considered before. Exploring, messing around in the world, getting our hands dirty – all of these enable us to make connections and see relationships that we would otherwise not have encountered and foster in us the willingness to try solutions that we would not otherwise have seen or thought about. Doing this effectively, as internationally recognised executive coach and author Aiko Bethea argues, is about how we show up for those we serve.

>  **GAME CHANGER INSIGHT**
>
> *'I think that there's so much about one having your own self-awareness about your own story, and who you are, and how you show up in the world.'*
>
> Aiko Bethea

Leadership always involves managing risk. For leaders who are naturally cautious by nature this can be daunting, to say the least. Such leaders, when confronted by risk, often shy away from creative and innovative thinking, which can lead to seemingly safe but outdated and poor decisions. Risk aversion can also be encouraged by conservative organisations. On the other hand, some leaders confronted by risk blindly continue to escalate their commitment, holding fast to a poor choice until they end up reinforcing defeat. The key is for leaders to be consistent and realistic in the way they manage risk. A successful decision is best, but in many circumstances even a bold yet unsuccessful decision may be better than no decision at all.

>  **ENCOUNTER AND RESPOND**
>
> How might you measure the nature and success of your decision-making and problem-solving practice in your school as a leader who focuses both your teams and the organisations which you serve?

# HOW CAN I BEST SERVE OTHERS?

## Intentional: The approach of leaders who focus

### Building shared purpose

From our work with schools around the world over the past decade, we have formed the view that the fundamental driver of the work of educators in bringing about improved outcomes for their learners comes down to purpose. In other words, if you know what your 'why' is you are much more likely to make the 'what' and 'how' happen.

In good schools people recognise that this simple understanding of the primacy of purpose belies the complex journey of exploration, encounter and discovery that characterises human development. While our books, charts and graphics tend to show life as a steady and constant stream of progress, often accompanied by arrows and steps, the reality of each life is (of course) much messier than this. Education is unlike any other business in this respect; no matter what we do, we cannot predict every stage and every outcome with precision. We know that certain things are likely to happen and can make provision for them. At different ages and stages of emotional, physical, intellectual, moral, social and spiritual development, students are probably more ready to take on learning of a specific kind. That does not guarantee that this learning will happen at a time and place of our choosing. Yet, with a combination of both experience and the judicious use of evidence, teachers and their leaders can come to develop a good understanding of what prompts, approaches and supports are most likely to help this to happen.

At different ages we want different things and our circumstances will influence the extent to which we will want to impose our own expectations for our children and their education. Parents' overarching desire for when their children are very young is for a safe and secure place in which they might learn and play in a manner that nurtures them and is resonant with the values of their family. As they grow older, we want our children to have friends who will support them and these values while they begin to seek the independence that is natural and normal for all children to want. By the final years of schooling, our attention focuses naturally on the immediate social context of learning and the question of what might come next for children who have become emerging adults with their own lives to lead.

There sits within all of this a quality of experience that many find hard to express at times. Quite naturally, stakeholders will often defer to the identification of quantifiable targets in the form of results. Such results do not, of themselves, constitute anything particularly negative. All human beings need achievement in their lives. Daniel Pink (2009) summarises the best of the international research in recent years to remind us that we are motivated first and foremost by the setting and attaining of tangible goals that boost our mastery, autonomy and purpose. The research of the Bill & Melinda Gates Foundation (2010) tells us that effective teachers secure excellent value-added results for their students as well as teaching them about the essential concepts of their fields.

However, educators will often and even habitually shy away from the hard edge of such measures without really appreciating that these benchmarks help families and the community to understand the growth and success of children throughout their schooling. It is far better for schools to predict what these measures might be and build a narrative for their community by contextualising them within the lives of the individuals and groups concerned. In this way, both the process and the product can be accounted for because both of them matter. We need to recognise that growth is both an experience and an outcome.

How does this play out in our conversations with our communities about our purpose – about what we stand for and how we will go about substantiating our values with intention and action? We know, for example, that in schools where sport and co-curricular achievement are important, parents will have expectations that their children will be provided with quality coaching and management, and that this will lead to the experience of victory. In the academic field, parents with a keen eye for social mobility, economic opportunity and the further educational pathways that might lead to realising these aspirations can and should have similar expectations that their children will get the best possible results. And every teacher has stories to tell about situations where a lack of balance in parents' approaches become evident, especially those parents whose love for their children becomes expressed unfortunately in forceful and unrealistic demands about numbers.

Should we, therefore, turn to the other extreme? The answer is not that simple. If an education is to be a proper rehearsal for the world that is to come, then removing numbers and grades is as unbalanced and unrealistic as the criticism that it seeks to address. It's a little bit like claiming that we prepare students for modern society when the learning ecosystem lacks the necessary degree of challenge and reward that our students will encounter in the technologically rich environment into which they will step the moment they leave school. This does not mean that we have to present a harsh or brutal reality to students; however, protecting them in a well-intentioned way from the need to develop both resilience and robustness in the face of adversity will undermine both the process and the product of learning. After all, if we are going to be resilient in our consensus around ethos, then we need to promote the resilience of those who form the consensus: students, staff, parents and other members of the extended school community.

## Building living history

We need to engage our community in an ongoing conversation about growth showing the concentric circles of community that develop around students themselves. We need to lead discussion about what matters to us and how we will express this in the fundamental written documents that will act as the formal and informal constitution or charter of the school. We need to explain how we will interact with each other to form relationships that will best promote our students' learning. We need to explain what we are doing and why we are doing it at every step of the way so that what we are doing can be both tested and validated.

We need to understand why families have chosen our school for their children and what they expect of us. At the same time, we need to talk with them about the road that lies ahead and show them how our experience can help them to prepare for this (and to sort things out when they go wrong). We need to understand from each other what is working and what is not working so that we can do what is essential: put the character, competency and wellness of the child first so that they might learn, live, lead and work in a way that will enable them to demonstrate the graduate outcomes of thriving in their world.

To do this we will need to construct with each other a living history of our school and its community that will allow the honourable traditions, accoutrement and customs of yesterday to be carried forward in a way that will bring reassurance of continuity with a treasured past. We will need to attend to all of the details of today so that school operations bring its community together to support the individual and collective needs that arise from its present educational setting and the demands that this places on everyone. Of particular importance here is the patience required when these demands seem to conflict with one other. And while the past and present are important, we cannot allow our schools to become trapped in them and tend only towards the minutiae of tests, swimming carnivals, uniforms and squabbles in the yard. We will need to project the work of the school forward to the future of its students and the communities that they will serve in the world of tomorrow with the patience and perspective that will place everything into its rightful context.

The social contract of a school, therefore, must cover the way in which its community achieves agreement about its purpose and how that will be brought about. In this way, our early learning, primary and secondary educational structures and systems work towards students using their emerging and well-grounded confidence in their capacity to claim a purpose for their lives, applying their learning and adaptive expertise to create solutions to the changing contexts of their lives and world according to this sense of purpose and also realising this purpose through strengthening their self-efficacy. Students should graduate equipped, empowered and enabled to thrive in their world.

We need to recognise and affirm that the purpose of school is to grow the character, competency and wellness of our students towards a specific end: taking responsibility for how they learn, live, lead and work by choosing a pathway to excellence for themselves that will shape their future and allow them to manage all of the inevitable triumphs, disasters and moments in between. When we talk about responsibility here, we're really talking about learner agency, as argued by David Price, educational thought leader and author of *The Power of Us*.

> **GAME CHANGER INSIGHT**
>
> *'What I mean by agency, I mean being more in control of your own life and the lives of your community and feeling that you can make a difference.'*
>
> **David Price**

With this sense of agency, learners will wrestle with both their inner drive to become and also the expectations of their family, friends, colleagues and broader community. By putting the needs of others before their own and leaning towards the needs of the future as their default, selflessness and forward-thinking become the prevailing characteristics of their approach. This in turn will help them to create the habits of reflection, gratitude and reciprocity that will strengthen their bonds with those around them and their place in society. They will learn to understand the mutually complementary roles of competition and collaboration as necessary aspects of human behaviour – and they will need to remain both curious and optimistic throughout.

**ENCOUNTER AND RESPOND**

We invite you to encounter and respond to a process of thinking differently about intentional leadership:

- What does being intentional as a leader and using shared purpose and living history look like in your school? What *should* it look like in your school?
- What could it mean to think differently about leading with intentionality in your context? What kinds of changes can you make to your leadership practice to support this?

## WHOSE AM I?

As leaders who focus, we need to encourage our schools and their stakeholders to perform so that we are consistently providing a whole education situated within the curriculum, co-curriculum, extracurricular pursuits and key relationships of a school community. This focus must be grounded in the agreed values and value proposition that drive a school towards the future that its students will inhabit.

> ### ⊙ ENCOUNTER AND RESPOND
>
> Are you a leader who focuses? We invite you to encounter the following reflective questions and respond to them by identifying two to three priorities for your own professional learning and the growth of your adaptive expertise and self-efficacy as a leader who focuses:
>
> - How do I ensure that change processes and initiatives are carefully designed and paced, and rigorously monitored?
> - How do I help my school to become a future-ready and future-fit community of inquiry and practice that uses evidence-informed decision-making processes and the best possible approaches to continuously evaluate its performance?
> - How do I develop the routines and processes to ensure that everything we do focuses the stated strategic intent of the school?
> - How do I create and embed the best means possible to measure how well students are gaining the knowledge, skills and learning habits for character, competency and wellness they need to succeed and thrive?
> - How do I develop the educational pathways and personalisation that support and challenge each student to succeed and thrive?

The fundamentals of performance in a school must be strong and the school community must know it is doing a good job. At the same time, they need to envision more than this. They need to be inspired to work together to improve the fundamentals and to seek better outcomes for more students by doing a great job. In the next chapter we will move from the fundamentals of a good school to the quest to become a great school by looking at leadership that aligns.

# CHAPTER 6
# Leadership that aligns

## STRATEGY, CULTURE AND REPUTATION: INTRODUCING LEADERSHIP THAT ALIGNS

As we generate strategy and lead towards the preferred future of our schools we build community. We need to align this community – to purpose, to people, place and planet, to practice. Time and again, members of school communities around the world tell us that leadership characterised by high trust and strong intent is what achieves this. Values-based, relational leadership styles promote openness and both the accepting and the taking of responsibility. This establishes commitment to common aspirations; a willingness to develop appropriate resourcing for the long-term success of a school and its community; a commitment to strategy, connected culture and supportive community that are always moving forward to a preferred future; and a distinctive culture that perpetuates the values and value propositions of that school.

Though it is a reality that all schools should and do have a corporate culture, we do not like to think of ourselves as corporate. We do not like to think of ourselves as a business. We are educators; we teach children. Yet all schools are businesses. Our core business is the task of improving outcomes for students by creating today's learning for tomorrow's world. At the same time, we do this in a manner that is uniquely relational, efficient and affordable. There is no other business like the business of educating students in schools, and the strategy, culture and community need to reflect what matters most in this type of business: the social enterprise of learning.

All schools should be able to articulate and measure their success in creating the culture of the social enterprise of learning and perpetuating an honest reputation about how well they do this. All members of a school have a responsibility to learn about, align themselves with and contribute to the health of the school community, its culture and its reputation. They also need to be able to respond and act decisively and constructively when the school needs change or development. Development or change in school culture may be the key responsibility of the principal, but all staff, students, families, partners and board members are critical influences too. All have a part to play in ensuring that the explicit goals and social contract inherent within their school's vision are met such that a good reputation ensues.

In asking and answering questions such as these, we must take care to construct and protect an authentic reputation that is based on worthy collective priorities as opposed to the leader's individual desire to be liked and popular. What does the school see as its community? How important is that community to the school and its aspirations? What processes are available to develop its reputation for seeking out the best strategies for creating today's learning for tomorrow's world? How do roles within that school combine to ensure some synergy of commitment to this restless and forward-looking leadership?

And right now, in this time of global disruption and educational change, part of our role as leaders who align is to align our schools to the times. We need to gather and learn together from our present circumstances to inject energy and vitality into actions that take advantage of the opportunities that are being presented – opportunities to be game changers. David Ferguson, headmaster of Westlake Boys High School in Auckland, New Zealand, offers the following reminder of this subject.

> # GAME CHANGER INSIGHT
>
> *'I think that unless we stop and talk about the experience that we've had and what it might mean we will just fall into exactly what we did previously because that's what we're used to. It's our default position ... More so now than ever, I think stopping and talking about why we're doing school and what we should be doing feels like probably the biggest priority.'*
>
> **David Ferguson**

Cultivating the relationship between people, purpose, strategy, culture and the reputation that these engender is, therefore, one of the key functions of a leader who aligns. It requires a significant quantum of both big-picture thinking and attention to detail. We need to show leadership styles that combine forethought and courage with creativity, subtlety and patience. We need a good understanding of the way teams function so we can get the most from and enjoy leading them. We need to explore how we can design and shape the high-performance culture of these teams (and the broader community) to help individuals become the best versions of themselves and to ensure that they can come together to deliver on the strategy and preferred future in a powerful and ethical fashion.

In this chapter, we look at the leadership competency of aligning. In 'Who am I?' we will explore the influence of belonging and shared intent on the character and purpose of responsible citizens. In 'Where do I fit in?' we will discuss the development and practice of leadership style. We will reflect on a strategic approach that blends an understanding of high-performance culture and school planning to turn possibility into reality in 'How can I best serve others?' Finally, you will have the opportunity to respond to the question 'Whose am I?' by thinking through how you bring your own value in the leadership that aligns to your school community.

# WHO AM I?

## Responsible citizens: The character of leaders who align

All schools and the teams within them are built on a foundation of belonging. What we do in education is intrinsically human centred – it is an activity that grows people. We need to create schools that are the social vehicles for the alignment and fulfillment of purpose. If we want people to come together willingly to achieve shared goals in a fashion that both builds positive team culture and facilitates the growth and development of individuals, we need to understand, respect and pay attention to fundamental requirements for diversity, equity and inclusion. It starts with belonging.

Over the past decade of research and connection with schools across the globe, we have formed the view that the purpose of education is to help young people with the character, competency and wellness to thrive in the world. It's about a human-centred model of development which we call *The Pathway to Excellence.* Not only do we need to embark on this process of development ourselves, our model also calls on each of us to support each and every one of our colleagues as they embark on their own journey of exploration, encounter and discovery.

Individually and together, therefore, we can be equipped, empowered and enabled on The Pathway to Excellence to build the civic character of belonging, the performance character of the achievement of potential, and the moral character of doing what is good and right in the world. In doing this, we need to feel as though we belong before we can achieve our potential. If we feel as though we belong and are achieving our potential, then we are more likely to do what is good and right in the world. It all starts with belonging.

We know that there are ongoing barriers to belonging in our world for learners. These obstacles can imposed by people, structures and systems that perpetuate discrimination on the basis of ethnicity, age, religion, disability, identity, gender and sexual orientation. We also know that when people are prevented – by either the choices of others or the structures and systems of society – from belonging, achieving their potential and doing what is good and right, we have an obligation to stand against this injustice. We believe that the ongoing mission at a School for tomorrow. reflects our fundamental belief that all people deserve fairness and justice in their lives. We also believe that everyone everywhere benefits from educational systems and structures that put into practice principles that create the conditions in which every person can learn, live, lead and work. School, therefore, should help individuals and those around them to belong, achieve their potential and do what is good and right. It should be a place of belonging where everyone is valued, respected and able to reach their inherent possibility.

We need to welcome people of all ethnicities, ages, religions, abilities, identities, genders and sexual orientations. We need to believe in and honour their distinct and diverse perspectives. We need to listen to their personal stories and use these to ensure our schools become more vibrant, creative learning places that drive our innovation and the hope of humanity. We need to recognise that our collective strength comes from the visible and invisible qualities that make each person remarkable. We need to commit to aligning our ethos, strategy, culture and business practices to ensure that schools are centres of belonging for all people. Ultimately people everywhere flourish when they feel loved, valued and known in equal measure through encountering others who believe in their inherent worth.

And so, our work as responsible citizens, the fifth graduate outcome of a school for tomorrow, starts with belonging: belonging for each person and for every team in pursuit of today's learning for tomorrow's world. Let's now consider what that looks like as we learn, live, lead and work as game changers.

## Learn

Responsible citizens are sincere contributors who are prepared to put the common interest and the needs of others before themselves. Inspired by service, they have a balanced perspective that is informed by their desire to create belonging, achieve potential and do what is good and right. They do this in ways that bring both value and values to enterprises including business, joint ventures, service entities, government and not-for-profit organisations in local, regional and global contexts.

## Live

They are dedicated to serving others. They use a positive approach, a sense of greater purpose and a long-term vision to encourage others to drive activity beyond their own immediate concerns to a shared intent. They give hope to others to discern and meet their responsibilities with assuredness.

## Lead

They contribute positively to their communities. They appreciate that citizenship competency involves balancing local, regional and global perspectives and intent through recognising, identifying with and contributing to different communities. This relies on the capacity to appreciate the rights and responsibilities that flow from interconnected social, cultural, economic and environmental contexts.

## Work

Finally, their work is grounded in acquiring knowledge of the needs of others and how best to meet those needs; gaining skills in discerning pathways, systems and processes that grow others and nurture their environment on a journey towards a preferred future; nurturing a disposition towards promoting shared goals and culture over personal ambitions; and building the capacity to reflect on the balanced perspective of their citizenship.

## Building strategy: The purpose of leaders who align

Successful leaders in schools recognise the need for a strategically envisioned and operationally aligned community. We have observed in our work that they are typically and inherently dissatisfied with the status quo and seek to redesign – or at least renovate – the structures and processes required to realise the vision and direction of a great school committed to graduating responsible citizens.

They employ a balanced perspective to make choices about investing hope, resources and significant commitment into research and development by planning, conducting and evaluating intentional projects and initiatives that are aligned to their school's shared intent to graduate young people who will thrive in their world. They do what they say they will do. They are guided by a common understanding of the close and mutually supportive relationship between their strategic vision, leadership, operations, governance and culture. They are clear about their own intent and what they do is aligned with this sense of purpose. They reinforce strategic clarity and connection in school activity by aligning school culture with strategy and translating this into daily operations, particularly in terms of their capacity to graduate responsible citizens.

Leaders who align also know that a school with a clear vision for its future and a set of plans that shows how this vision can be achieved is best placed to do what it wants to do. That school's agreed purpose and meaning help its community to grow together and strive for an agreed set of goals. It is capable of putting into place the realistic changes necessary for this growth while protecting those enduring values and customs that help the school to define what it is. It can articulate the culture of leadership and learning that will help its community members to behave in a way that supports the school's fundamental values.

Leaders who align also help communities develop a shared intent. Intent in a future-fit school is always about a conscious decision to travel in a specific direction. Implicitly or explicitly it is also about what we choose not to do instead. Intent brings a school confidence about how it will make progress at individual, group and whole-school levels. It helps us to balance the enduring needs from yesterday with the urgent needs of today and the long-term needs of tomorrow. If we lack clarity about what these choices are and how we can connect them with the daily life of all in the school, then we limit the possibilities for growing and developing together as a community of inquiry and practice.

So, how might we then approach the task of fostering the shared intent that is at the heart of strategy? We need to be able to see this articulated in a shared vocabulary and agree on the velocity at which it will be enacted. This will be expressed in publications and conversations every day in a deliberate, targeted and intentional fashion. Every such interaction will be taken as an opportunity to explain the 'why', the 'what' and the 'how' and to then engage stakeholders. This allows them to take on the agreed language and narrative, helping them to direct their own efforts towards building the vision. This intent needs to become more than simply aspirational. It needs to become part of culture, 'the way we do things here', without becoming so fixed in place that the process and product detract from the intended purpose.

However, leaders who align know that consensus is hard to attain and that there will always be critics within every group of stakeholders. Disagreement around the margins and periphery of the school experience is, of course, natural and essential. No human system is perfect. Importantly, without the input of those for whom the school experience is not working we lack the capacity to tell the truth about our school and what it is doing for its students, families, staff and community. Over time, leaders who align build the character of their schools to incorporate a willingness to engage in an honest assessment of their intent.

The following questions are a useful starting point for this type of reflection:

- What can we do to make this better?
- What can we do to move this forward?
- How resourceful can we be?
- How innovative, how original in our thinking can we be?
- What are the rewards for contribution?
- How will we deal with conflict?
- What will make way to allow us the time we need to do this together?

What we can do with these questions is help our schools think about its preferred future, the direction it needs to go in to reach this future, and the decisions that will need to be made along the way. If intent is who and what we want to become and action is what we will do to bring about this preferred future, then strategies are the choices we make about how we are going to get there and how we prioritise the allocation of the resources that we will need. Strategy provides the direction we need to make our intent a reality. It is the essential architecture of the solutions by which we may construct our preferred future. Good strategy asks us to anticipate the problems that we will face and the mechanisms, structures and systems that will bring a community together and align itself to the purpose for which its school exists. Great strategy covers all the bases, imagining those things that others might not see in the ordinary course of events.

This calls on leadership that is informed by research and evidence and it is shaped by judgement and experience. It recognises that past performance and corresponding habits should never be the default, but also that it is rare in the lives of humans that radical and revolutionary change, no matter how attractive to some, will be the right course of action. At the same time, we can't turn our backs on the world around us. The need for a technology-enriched learning ecosystem is a case in point. Eleni Kyritsis, deputy head of Junior School at Strathcona Girls Grammar School in Victoria, provides insight on this.

> **GAME CHANGER INSIGHT**
>
> 'Technology's not going to go away, as much as we want to think that it is. The more we embrace it and incorporate it in our education system, the more it will support our students. They're using it no matter what. They're going to have it at home. They're going to have it when they're out in the big world. So, it's about us showing them how to use it in the right way and also showing them the potential of what can come from technology ... It's all around us in everything we do, every day ... So, we have to embrace that and go with it. To lock it out of schools is not doing justice for any students, really.'
>
> **Eleni Kyritsis**

If we are to conceive of an intent that helps us take the big step forward and up to honour today's learning for tomorrow's world, we need to dream big, make bold choices and then work out the little and larger steps that are going to get us there. And somewhere along the way, every school needs to work out how to measure whether it has become the school that it wants to be. Our job, as leaders who align, is to work out how to tie all of this together.

> **⏸ ENCOUNTER AND RESPOND**
>
> What defines your character and purpose as a leader who aligns your school community towards transformation through responsible citizenship?

# WHERE DO I FIT IN?

## The practice of leaders who align

Each one of us must develop a range of leadership styles that enable us to connect with, motivate, engage, direct and inspire the participation of our teams and organisations. Your leadership styles should enable you to align people with purpose and practice to obtain their willing support and the confidence, loyalty, trust and respect required to learn, live, lead and work together with success. Tables 6.1 and 6.2 show what this might mean for you at team and organisational levels.

### Table 6.1: Aligning as a leader of a team

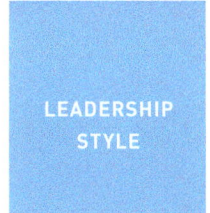

| LEADERSHIP STYLE | Demonstrates understanding of motivation, integrity, courage, compassion and humility in applying a range of effective personal approaches to leadership. |
| --- | --- |
| | Adopts effective balance of participative and motivating behaviours in making decisions and influencing the team to achieve the desired results. |

### Table 6.1: Aligning as a leader of an organisation

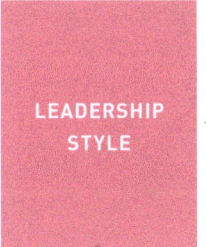

| LEADERSHIP STYLE | Discerns and makes sense of what is going on within teams and other cultural and structural groupings of the organisation. |
| --- | --- |
| | Uses political skill appropriately to prepare thoroughly, secure resources, achieve goals, remove constraints, align team members and build support without compromising personal ethical standards or school values. |

## Leadership style

Successful leaders continually craft and refine their leadership styles: the tone they use, the way they communicate, and the structures and processes that they create to align those around them honestly and earnestly to the mission of their team and school. Throughout this process, you need to be yourself. Your leadership styles must be authentic. They must flow from both your values and also the imperative of the task to which you are called. Thus, it's not about being a chameleon or about gaining popularity for its own sake. And it's certainly not about manipulating others or the moment by pretending to be something that you are not. It's about adapting your approach so that you can empathise with others, support their needs and understand their potential to contribute – all while maintaining your focus on what matters most: today's learning for tomorrow's world.

An ongoing process of introspection and consultation will allow you to examine the impact and suitability of your leadership styles in different situations. It will also allow you to consider how you can align yourself and others to the values that guide your actions while also allowing for personal growth and development over time. Leadership styles should remain fluid in their articulation while always being grounded in the values and value proposition for which you stand – values that embrace all community stakeholders when forming a shared vision, as Pernille Ripp, Danish educator and prolific author, articulates in a single question.

### GAME CHANGER INSIGHT

*'Whose voice is missing and how is that impacting our understanding of the world?'*

Pernille Ripp

Preparing a leadership style asks you to consider and balance two types of leadership behaviour – participatory and motivating – with which you can encourage followers to dedicate themselves towards realising a shared vision or task. Participatory, or engaging, leadership behaviour influences people to engage or participate in a process, either through collaborating with you or following your directions. It is a reasonably straightforward approach that asks people to risk little for a moderate return. Leaders who align do so by establishing what is expected in practice in the first instance. By and large, people are happy to fall in line with what is asked of them and may even do what they are told, but they may not be willing to do much more beyond the basics of what has been established in exchange for a predictable and reasonable rate of reward. Relationships can be friendly and professional at the same time, but rarely, if ever, do they go beyond the confines of work. Training establishes what is expected and trainees seek to replicate what is shown to them. Their expertise may grow with experience, but that expertise is rarely adaptive in nature. Over time, as people string together a series of individual and collective wins, they become increasingly likely to stay the course because of the evidence of performance and success. Participatory leadership is a more transactional approach that can support the development of a series of standard operating procedures that form the basis of the desirable behaviours underpinning team culture. It can also lead to a willingness to entertain a leadership style based more on motivating leadership.

Leading through motivating behaviour takes this all a significant step further. It asks people to commit to a process that is much more purpose-driven in nature and will ultimately be transformative. Leaders who align, therefore, can use motivating behaviour to align people to purpose and then develop shared norms of practice to support that purpose. By acting willingly in accordance with this shared rationale for the nature of the enterprise and the need to go beyond normal levels of performance in the spirit of continuous improvement, team members can be encouraged to sacrifice short-term self-interest for the sake of their team and personal sense of fulfillment. Meanwhile, they will develop adaptive expertise and self-efficacy that see them willing to become the best versions of themselves, not just doing a job to a certain level of technical proficiency. They will also become motivated externally by the incentive of long-term consequences that reward positive intent and action and also demonstrate the likely negative impact of inaction or a choice not to involve themselves in the enterprise. More is risked in return for this reward and the 'ask', the point at which individuals are invited to assist in the process through their contributions or sacrifices, tends to occur at a time when evidence isn't yet available to demonstrate tangible success. It can take a leap of faith to commit and you should not be surprised if some potential followers and collaborators are not ready to make this decision or are less inclined to take the risk.

Your leadership styles will involve using both participatory and motivating behaviours in different circumstances to make decisions and influence your team to achieve the desired results. Experience will help you to know which of these works well under what circumstances. Use mentors and role models. Study leadership in theory and in action. Imitate what you see as great leadership, so long as you adapt it to the particular needs of your own situation. Studying the work of others can help you to develop a portfolio of different participatory and motivational approaches to leadership that can equip you to understand and shape your team's culture and environment for the better in a whole range of contexts. It can ensure that you are effectively prepared for assuming the responsibilities of leading others and managing the resources allocated to you with wisdom and care.

You can also learn much by deliberately shying away from what you think are poor examples of leaders who align. When you do so, however, make sure that you understand the reasons why you do not approve of this leadership. Be careful of the example of leaders who use mostly participatory behaviour to get their team onside. While this can promote group cohesion and make the leader popular, it can also lead to the performance of the group not lifting when necessary and the stagnation of values and team culture. On the other hand, leaders who use mostly motivating behaviour can create a team environment where team members do not have enough of their social needs met, which in turn can leave them feeling distant from their team's purpose, ethos and leader. As ever, there is a balancing act to be performed. It's unlikely that any approach will ever be 100 per cent right or effective, but over time you can hone your judgement and skills so that you can help more people to align themselves to purpose while also helping your team and organisation align themselves with their people.

Finally, tone is important. If we teach who we are and we lead from the core of our being, how we practise our professional kindnesses and our public professional discourse should matter as much to us as how kind we are to the children in our care. We believe that in many ways it is the quality of our welcome and the manners that underpin that welcome, the depth of sincerity about our commitment to the belonging of others, the thoughtfulness of our communication and our openness to ideas and situations that will determine the success of our leadership styles. As leaders who align, we can't forget the need to align ourselves to the greater purpose and the people this purpose serves. We can't allow ourselves to become complacent or caught in a rut. We need to continue to challenge ourselves by asking this essential question: does the character of our relationships reflect the character of belonging that enables us to create today's learning for tomorrow's world?

## ⏸ ENCOUNTER AND RESPOND

How might you measure the nature and success of your leadership style practice in your school as a leader who aligns both your teams and the organisations that you serve?

# HOW CAN I BEST SERVE OTHERS?

## Strategy: The approach of leaders who align

Leaders who align with success go beyond aligning themselves with their people. They use the trust and credibility built up through the exercise of leadership styles within positive relationships to direct their communities of inquiry and practice towards the strategies that will improve outcomes for learners and help them to thrive in their world.

Every school needs to know where it's going, why it's going there and how it's going to get there. Every school needs a plan to turn well-intentioned wishful thinking into a well-thought-out, well-constructed and well-regarded road map about how it will reach this preferred-future state. Every school needs to make decisions about what's really important and what it will and won't do to bring this plan to life. Strategy gives us direction. It allows each of us to connect our own stories to the compelling narrative of yesterday, today and tomorrow that creates the shared enterprise of a school and positively impacts society at large. Mark Hutchinson offers relevant thoughts on this.

> ## GAME CHANGER INSIGHT
>
> *'Schools are incredibly important social institutions for the leverage that they provide on bringing about adaptation to social change and helping families engage with their communities.'*
>
> **Professor Mark Hutchinson**

Think about your story. Where did you begin? Who are you now? Where are you going? Strategy is part of this story, a way of connecting your past, your present and your future. It provides a way of taking you from where you are now to where you want to be in the future. In this sense, your strategy is your plan to go in the right direction to achieve your vision and make your story end the way that you want it to end. Thinking strategically means thinking about your story and identifying the similarities and differences between who you are now and who you want to be in the future (your outcomes). It means working out a plan of action to nurture and maintain the similarities while addressing the gaps created by the differences. It also involves thinking clearly about the most important things that you can do to make your story move in the right direction: the critical ideas that define or characterise your direction and plan (strategies), the detailed planning and actions that will help you move in the right direction (operations) and the resources you will need to implement these actions.

Schools that are seriously committed to becoming great schools therefore need to do more than simply replicate solid performance in the basic foundations of building a future-fit education. They must identify the secret sauce of high-performance culture, foster the leadership to perpetuate it and re-engineer structures and systems. This is specifically in order for the efforts of their faculty to be motivated, influenced, directed and inspired towards learning and teaching that is shaped by a curriculum embedding character, competency and wellness in a deliberate, targeted and intentional fashion.

Figure 6.1: The equip–empower–enable model – the secret sauce of high-performance learning

What is this secret sauce? How can a school assemble the right ingredients for high-performance culture in a whole education? At a School for tomorrow. we talk about equipping learners to locate their voice, empowering them to demonstrate agency and enabling them to exercise advocacy. These qualities – which form the equip–empower–enable model illustrated in figure 6.1 – are fuelled by the development of an adaptive expertise and self-efficacy that in turn generate a willingness to fulfil a sense of purpose characterised by both selflessness and the pursuit of excellence. With this model as our base, we can now step through the ingredients of this secret sauce of learning, living, leading and working together in a community of inquiry and practice to equip, empower and enable learners to thrive in their world.

There are three key ingredients with which we need to equip our students: aspirations, a sense of kinship and pathways to success. With these in place, we can empower students by helping them to feel they belong to and are engaged in a school that keeps them in their groove and holds them to their educational purpose – the pursuit of excellence through character. We then enable students to do this by consciously crafting relationships, at all levels, that inspire, challenge and support them every day to demonstrate the character, competency and wellness to achieve the graduate outcomes towards which all learning in their school is directed.

What is the work required to develop and maintain the high-performance culture with which game changers can equip, empower and enable their learning community with this secret sauce? Perhaps it might be helpful to think of the following as steps in the cooking method:

- the learning work – identifying a rationale, model and trajectory for the high-performance learning culture that drives the work of a great school
- the imperative for student competency – building student voice, agency and fluency in character and competency by designing and creating the learning culture, formative impacts and guiding narratives that foster development and lead to the attainment of desired graduate educational outcomes
- the imperative for staff competency – identifying a model for adult learning and change that multiplies the transformative moments and ongoing professional learning journeys that lead to staff growth in corresponding learning, teaching and leadership for character, competency and wellness
- the role of a community of inquiry and practice – shaping the adaptive expertise, self-efficacy and aligned purpose of staff in a community of inquiry and practice dedicated to improved outcomes for learners in character, competency and wellness
- the impact of strategy and systems – determining and operationalising a strategic educational intent for a community of inquiry and practice through designing, planning and implementing whole-school, high-performance professional learning for staff, performance-development programs and support systems
- the habits of learners – promoting a tendency towards curiosity and inquiry, a passion for improvement through change and a commitment to the research activity (expressed through priorities, pilots, projects and personalised plans) that creates the evolving evidence basis for high-performance learning culture

- the path to competency through relationship – strengthening adaptive expertise and self-efficacy in learning, teaching and leadership character and competency through the pedagogies of character apprenticeship
- the measure of great educators – evaluating the journey towards high-performance learning culture by measuring growth in individual development, program delivery and organisational maturity.

We can share three broad observations about how great schools go about using these steps to create high-performance educational culture. The first is that the deliberate, targeted and intentional centrality of providing a whole education for character, competency and wellness is at the heart of a future-fit education. Internationally there is an emerging industry standard to routinely meet and exceed expectations of stakeholders for outstanding educational outcomes for learners. Further, the language of stakeholders is typically overwhelmingly expressed in terms of the development of the whole person and the character, competencies and wellness that comprise this. With this insight in mind, schools should apply themselves to demonstrating the habits, routines and traditions of whole education routinely and consistently in their daily practice at both their highest and most mundane of levels. These can in turn create and nurture a culture that might subsequently be transformed through the equip–empower–enable secret sauce into high-performance learning culture. One cautionary understanding that we can make about this (as we referred to previously) is that habits of the status quo and perceived traditions themselves can and often do inhibit schools from taking the big step forward and up to becoming a great school.

Our second observation is that the equip–empower–enable secret sauce of high-performance learning culture can also drive how a school meets stakeholder expectations. Stakeholders in schools believe that school culture, climate and ethos are a significant condition of and contributor to school performance and student achievement. How this translates to success for students through their learning journeys is important. Student learning journeys are best defined as the ways in which students travel along their educational pathways. As they do, they form relationships with teachers and their peers, and they experience learning through the programs and events of an evidence-based and research-driven curriculum for character learning. In time, students grow and make progress with increasing confidence and success. School communities and their leaders need to develop school culture, climate and ethos that sustain these journeys in a positive fashion evidenced by both school performance and student achievement. These results need to be fed back to the community and warranted in the practice of expert teachers.

Our third observation on this topic is that the purpose and relationality of the character of a leader and a leader of character in a school should be directed towards achieving the purpose and culture of a whole education. Leaders help in the first instance to identify and model norms of character, competency and wellness for the students and families in their communities. Leaders can also nurture the conditions that encourage significant momentum in cultivating the ingredients of the equip–empower–enable secret sauce for growing the whole person. Lastly, leaders encourage and safeguard the standards for implementing successful culture, the method by which this secret sauce continuously improves in a future-fit community of inquiry and practice.

Schools who want to build high-performance learning culture should concentrate their attention most keenly on doing those things that really count towards growing their organisational maturity as future-fit schools. To do this, they first need to think about and assess their overall capacity in character education by tracking the trajectories of their students' learning experiences within a whole education. At the same time, they need to assess the attainment of their graduate outcomes and the character, competencies and wellness of their students in keeping with these outcomes. They also need to reflect on the character learning in theory and practice through which the potential of students to achieve these outcomes might be optimised.

How might we generate and align our community towards a high-performance learning culture that earns and maintains the reputation that we want for our school? Strategy, marketing and communications are very important. Yet it is the way we relate to, connect with and achieve a shared purpose with the people in our schools that is most critical to our reputation. In other words, reputation is about people. Reputation rises and falls depending on the culture that is built within a school. It depends on the quality of the people in our community and the extent to which they are prepared to adopt and grow the culture of their school in alignment with the strategic intent of the organisation. This applies as much to individuals as it does to groups and whole entities.

In a relational industry such as ours, we are often judged by how people feel cared for by others. As leaders who seek to align with people and help them to align with us and each other, we are often faced with challenging questions about the nature of this care. Did the school meet the expectations it established? Was the school able to achieve the outcomes it said it would?

Have the students grown in the way that they should have? Have the quality of our teams and the commitment they exhibit to our shared purpose, on both personal and professional levels, made the difference? Will our reputation spread through word of mouth the way we would like it to? As ever, there are further questions to guide the key elements of our ongoing process of inquiry:

- Are we future-focused? Is our school inspired by the possibilities of the future for our learners?

- Is our practice character-rich? Does our school have a set of graduate outcomes that define its expectations for the character, competencies and wellness of its learners?

- Is our work action-oriented? Do our teachers focus on continually improving outcomes for our learners?

- Are our communities inclusive and empowering? Do we listen carefully for the voices of all of our stakeholders in thinking through aspirations, kinship and pathways to success for all learners?

- Is our inquiry reflective? How consistently do students, teachers, leaders and school teams reflect on what they are doing to contribute towards the achievement of graduate outcomes by every learner?

Progress towards realising this secret sauce is never fixed. Even the very best schools are never perfect in striving for their goals. We all want to conserve what is enduringly valuable while seeking the best that innovation can offer. Achieving this balance is an ongoing quest.

## Planning

School planning is a structured approach to ensuring that a school aligns its ethos to its strategy to its operations. This is to ensure that it is achieving its purpose and responding to the need for its own version of the secret sauce of high-performance culture. Planning is an essential step that a school should take in implementing a cycle of school improvement. School improvement begins with reflection on and articulation of key values and relationships. These values inform the development of a school's culture of leadership and learning.

A school plan consists of the documents that provide a school with its vision for its future and the means by which its desired culture can be created from that vision. It is generated through research, consultation, development, piloting, implementation and review. It contains the most important educational, architectural, financial, strategic and operational decisions about a school as it moves through the next stage of its story.

To meet all of these needs and provide relevant guidance to improve all facets of school communities, school plans are made up of many related components. These include:

- School strategy

A school strategy is a road map for realising a school's preferred future. It comprises a handful of key decisions about the direction the school will take over a coming period of time – usually three to five years.

- Strategic plan

This is the document that provides a school with its vision for its future and articulates the key decisions that must be implemented for it to achieve its desired culture and outcomes. A strategic plan will usually outline the community's philosophy, ethos and vision for its preferred future, as well as the strategies that must be implemented to bring these to life. Sometimes this document will also include measures and case studies.

- Operational plan

An operational plan is a comprehensive plan enabling a school to implement its strategic plan through an aligned set of operational goals, the primary responsibility for which is allocated to specific school teams.

- Action plans

These documents translate a school's operational plan into plans for individual faculty or project teams who will take responsibility for the achievement of goals. There will also often be action plans for individual staff members, aligning personal goals with their school's strategic and operational plans.

- Master plan

A master plan is a school's long-term plan for using its physical environment to achieve its strategic intent.

- Financial plan

A school's financial plan includes its long-term approach for managing its finances to achieve its strategic intent.

Responsibility for different aspects of a school plan will cascade down from the board to the leadership team and principal to middle leaders and to individual staff members, depending on who has carriage of which aspect of the plan under the school's approach to governance.

United Make is an experimental think tank and multidisciplinary studio that explores design through the act of making. Founder and director Mond Qu offers a valuable perspective on how the intentionality of a plan's design can support our aspirations.

> **GAME CHANGER INSIGHT**
>
> *'The ability to understand that design is a way of thinking about the future.'*
>
> Mond Qu

Schools around the world have become very good at developing strategic planning documents that rely on community consultation to establish such things as values, vision, mission and strategy. We encourage you to consider how to work together with stakeholders to bring these documents to life through intentional design. After all, having a well-designed statement and accompanying plan is one thing – converting it into a known and lived experience in the community is another.

As a leader, you can use the 5D approach first detailed in Chapter 3 (page 78) to put all these elements of a school plan in place:

1. Discover the most relevant data about the school and/or team journey and its stakeholders' sense of belonging and connection to the actual educational experience of the school.
2. Diagnose the patterns you are seeing in the data, which will allow you to tell a true story of yesterday, today and tomorrow.
3. Decide what needs to be done to create a preferred future and the strategy to build it.
4. Design a solution for reaching the preferred future together. This includes the likely steps required to make this happen, the desired culture that will support the achievement of these steps and the shape and character of the ecosystem that will house this culture.
5. Deploy a range of plans and initiatives that will define the key milestones and the flow of daily life in key areas of operations as the community proceeds toward making its vision happen.

> **⚡ ENCOUNTER AND RESPOND**
>
> We invite you to encounter and respond to a process of thinking differently about being strategic about high-performance culture as a leader:
>
> - What does being strategic about high-performance culture as a leader look like in your school? What *should* it look like in your school? Respond by collecting a series of images and keywords, which may also include original drawings and text, that best articulate your vision for high performance.
>
> - What could it mean to think differently about being strategic with your leadership in your context? What kinds of changes can you make to your leadership practice to support this?

## WHOSE AM I?

Aligning as a leader means creating a direct correlation between vision, intention, means and outcome and the people who will live through these phenomena and experiences. We need to know, in our school communities, what our preferred future is, the strategy that will define the key choices we will make to reach that future and how that will work on a daily basis.

> **⏸ ENCOUNTER AND RESPOND**
>
> Are you a leader who aligns? We invite you to encounter the following reflective questions and respond to them by identifying two to three priorities for your own professional learning and the growth of your adaptive expertise and self-efficacy as a leader who aligns:
>
> - How am I a servant leader who builds trust in the culture and relationships of the community?
>
> - How do I set direction for professional standards and accountability, within a model that balances high expectation and feedback with support and recognition?
>
> - How do I foster a professional culture in which constructive and critical feedback about school programs, administration and leadership is welcomed, and grounded in shared respect and appreciation?
>
> - How do I ensure that all stakeholders in my school community have appropriate roles to play as partners and co-creators in the future of the school and its trajectory?
>
> - How do I ensure that my school is well-resourced and structured as it drives towards its vision and meets its goals?

Aligning from a team perspective means understanding what needs to be done to influence the culture and behaviours of the people who comprise the team. It is a question of how best to bind them together constructively so that all perform their roles to the highest possible standards and become together more than just the convergence of a group of disparate individuals – so that they become a team committed to each other and to their cause to the extent that they will sacrifice self-interest for the sake of each other. Aligning from an individual level is as much about how an individual's sense of identity is formed through a process of personal growth in character, competency and wellness as it is a deliberate response to the vision and values, and the purpose and practice of the community to which an individual belongs. Leadership that aligns is therefore about how 'my purpose' becomes 'our purpose' through a deep understanding of how to serve 'our people', 'our place' and 'our planet'. This is how individual preference and ambition becomes collective intent: through the application of styles and approaches of leadership to the creation of team culture, standards and reputation that in turn shape 'our practice'. It is this sense of collaboration in a community of inquiry and practice that is inspired by leadership that enriches, which we will explore in the next chapter.

# CHAPTER 7
# Leadership that enriches

## CONNECTION THROUGH TEAMS: INTRODUCING THE LEADERSHIP THAT ENRICHES

Outside of the family, school is the predominant social structure our society has evolved and approved to achieve the critical task of educating children to be ready for a future spent learning, living, leading and working in the world. For all of the faults that we may perceive, the idea of school and the systems and operations that underpin it have endured because we value this social function. At its most basic, school is the social vehicle through which young people are equipped, empowered and enabled by older people. In our opinion, we most likely perpetuate it because, despite others' suggestions, we want and need school to act as that point of connection so that we can, in the words of our colleague and game changer Leann Wilson, 'learn from others, learn with others, do it ourselves, and share with others'.

School is thus always about both us and others. This should not surprise us as educators and leaders. We know that as humans we are meant (for the most part) to learn, live, lead and work in community with each other. As we go about our lives, therefore, we form and are formed (either formally or informally) into groups. They're so very important to us in confirming the essence of our shared humanity. They help us to socialise, make friends and receive support, achieve our tasks, and promote social cohesion and positive behaviours. In schools, these behaviours comprise the character, competency and wellness that we aspire to for our students and all other members of the community that we serve.

All groups function in similar ways. While the context and culture of groups can and do create important distinctions that form identity, much of what each team does is very similar to what occurs in other groups. In other words, while the specifics of human personality can seem unique, human behaviour collectively is rarely so distinctive, although the minutiae of context (particularly when imbued with the emotion that shared history and meaning can bring) may make it seem so.

Groups function best when they have a common goal supported by a cohesive effort. When groups share a purpose or mission they start to become teams. This mission aligns their intentions and actions, focusing their work on attaining an agreed set of outcomes that establishes the team's vision. Team members share purpose, strategy and culture while performing complementary roles. Each of us will have a different role to play according to the purpose, time, place and composition of our group. Group members' mutual respect for and understanding of each other is important.

Almost all people actively seek membership of small groups and, as we've noted, groups can be converted into teams when they share a purpose. Why should this happen? Teams harness the talents of individuals and provide greater social satisfaction for members through the resulting sense of belonging and ability to fulfil potential – this is in addition to the propensity teams have for supporting members to do good and right. In other words, teams build character together. They make possible – through the pooling of competencies and resources, and the mutual support provided for wellness – that which could not be done by individuals working by themselves. As human beings, we recognise and appreciate these advantages and we seek to take advantage of them. That's why we want to be involved in teams – especially effective teams.

Recognising and shaping individual and group behaviour to form teams is essential for your success as a leader who enriches. There are some basic ideas about team development that you know already help you manage your team's actions and behaviour towards achieving these outcomes: building interdependency; establishing common purpose, standards, culture and processes (especially decision-making); mentoring and coaching individuals for success; preparing teams for the need for change; and implementing systems of review and renewal. You will also know of the importance of defining a vision, establishing a clear plan and coherent structures, and defining goals. We have talked in this book already about delegation, supervision and feedback. We will canvas conflict resolution later in this chapter.

Connection is the basic task of team leadership. No matter our role in schools, no matter the scope of our roles and no matter how grand our ideas are, we need to connect people through teams. If we want to be effective as leaders on any level, we need to work at the capabilities involved in performing this task. The success of any educational venture depends on our ability to do these things by connecting people to the notion that working for and with each other is better than working for and by ourselves. Debbie Dunwoody reminds us of this.

> **GAME CHANGER INSIGHT**
>
> '... that notion of "we're all here to contribute to something bigger than ourselves" and that notion of "service" is really important ... that's something that we hold true, and I hold true personally, to what an education in preparing someone for the future is all about.'
>
> **Debbie Dunwoody**

We know that individuals can and should be enriched by the fellowship of others. We believe that leading through teams enhances the whole school by empowering people in this way. This is characterised by team creation that consciously acknowledges the dignity, worth and agency of individuals within the community of inquiry and practice. At the heart of this needs to be our commitment to the notion that every human is home to a unique life, one that should merit the honour and respect of others.

In this chapter we look at the leadership competency of enriching. In 'Who am I?' we will explore the nature of teams, building systems and operations in schools and the impact of this on the character and purpose of team creators. In 'Where do I fit in?' we will discuss the practice of team cultivation and conflict resolution. We will reflect on the collaborative approach that employs team design and fostering positive relationships to get the best out of teams in 'How can I best serve others?' Finally, you will have the opportunity to respond to the question 'Whose am I?' by thinking through how you bring your own value in leadership that enriches your school community.

# WHO AM I?

## Team creators: The character of leaders who enrich

The success of leaders depends in so many ways on their capacity to create and sustain teamwork in an environment of trust, support, interdependence and group effort. This is a complex and challenging task that requires the willing collaboration of capable, action-oriented individuals committed to a common purpose and with a strong sense of urgency and identification with their team. Teams work best when they are teams of leaders who can align their goals with the wider goals of the organisation, assume leadership when the circumstances demand and create structures and processes appropriate to the goals of the team and the personal characteristics of individuals within the team.

All teams have structures around which they operate. People who lead successful teams know and use these to their advantage. Constructing and nurturing a positive team structure begins with identifying the team's broadest goal and focusing on achieving this with the support of clear roles and accountabilities, effective communication, supervision and support that includes performance feedback based on objective judgement relative to established criteria for success.

Leaders who enrich form their teams under different circumstances. Leaders need to identify team members' strengths and weaknesses, make use of team members' knowledge and experience and, if possible, place them in positions and roles that best suit their abilities and personalities. They will need to reform their teams when there are changes in composition and roles can change when this happens.

Maintaining teams requires a practical approach that includes establishing a team vision with members and then continually referring to that vision and related defined goals. Team leadership is always reliant on leadership by example, something that is powerful in helping teams to set boundaries about what is and is not desirable or acceptable.

Successful teams are built on positive relationships in which team members enhance each other and work together towards the group's goal. Leaders of such teams respect the individuality, contexts and roles of group members, demonstrating the capacity to lead individuals while leading their team as a whole. Leaders must develop the ability to manage team members, evaluate their performance, make decisions about them and provide instructions and corrections that will affect them. They need to exercise skill, judgement and sensitivity in understanding individuals' dignity, hope, ambition, strengths, weaknesses and anxieties, remembering that individual differences in capability and personality account for so many observable individual behaviours. Understanding, mutual trust, respect and communication are the keystones to successful relationships for both team members and their leaders. This is about a deep consciousness of the other, as beautifully articulated by Eddie Woo, a secondary school teacher at Cherrybrook Technology High School, New South Wales, and YouTube education pioneer.

### GAME CHANGER INSIGHT

'One of my core convictions is that every individual, every human being I interact with is of infinite value. That's not an overstatement. That's actually the most accurate way that I can say, you know, this is a human being in front of me, who I have the opportunity and the privilege of helping to support in their learning, is worthy of all the time and attention and energy and devotion that I can give to them.'

**Eddie Woo**

Role and task allocation is important to ensure that ambitions are achieved without confusion about friendship and team roles. This is perhaps the hardest team relationship principle. People do not want their leaders to be aloof or arrogant, yet overfamiliarity can result in leaders who make decisions based purely on friendship or for the sake of popularity, rather than on balancing the needs of the task, the team or the individual. Teams appreciate leaders who can get the job done and who place the needs of others before themselves. Effective relationships can be maintained, without overfamiliarity, through mutual respect, understanding, fairness and courtesy. Personal humility and a good sense of humour on the part of the leader are essential in this as well. It is possible to join in the fun of the team, but this can never be the only factor at play.

Regular and effective communication institutes, develops and improves team relationships. Communication is achieved through words, presence, standards, behaviours and actions. Without adequate contact and communication it is difficult to establish a positive influence, develop sound relationships and exercise effective leadership. Leaders need to establish effective communication and encourage its use. They need to be conscious of never micromanaging or belittling an individual's contribution. Leaders need to value being honest and admitting to uncertainties and mistakes.

So, what can you do to create effective team relationships and communication? You need to work at knowing and being yourself. Whatever the situation, you need to strive to be fair, be firm and be friendly without being overly familiar – respect is far more important over time than popularity. It helps a great deal if you know your team members, their characters and their backgrounds well, and also avoid meddling unnecessarily in the affairs of the team. You need to encourage them to believe in themselves and their ability to do the task at hand. Praise them where they deserve it and be willing to take them aside and correct them when they have not performed in accordance with their abilities and tasks. It helps if you can project confidence and calmness – even when you may not necessarily feel these qualities yourself! And remember that you are never alone; you should be open to drawing on those around you for advice.

There is a very specific application of the cultural development of teams within a school's community of inquiry and practice. The culture work that sits at the heart of this is about ensuring the articulation and application of a school's whole program of education to build learners' capacity in character, competency and wellness through the work of the team. We can therefore measure the success of the team and the community by how students, teachers, leaders, teams and members of the broader community collaborate to do the learning work that improves outcomes for learners.

We can typically see this enacted in the rigorous use of evidence-based and research-driven learning. The richness in relationships and the cultural capital that arise from this will amplify the strategic depth and distribution of leadership throughout the school. The quality and consistency of the performance that arises from the shared work of the community in acquiring that disposition towards inquiry that allows them to ask the right questions and to form balanced and insightful answers to them will allow all to benefit from practice that relies on collaborative wisdom about what really works.

Our work as team creators is about connecting people to purpose through practice. Let's explore what it looks like to learn, live, lead and work as a team creator, the sixth and final graduate outcome of a school for tomorrow.

### Learn

Team creators know how to build and work well within teams. Inspired by relationality, they have the ability to create human-centred and diverse collaboration meaningfully, compassionately and productively in ways that bring out the best outcomes for all of us.

### Live

They are inspired to become honourable colleagues who recognise our common humanity and work to enhance it. They use respect, kindness, diversity, equity, inclusion and appreciation for individual enterprise and shared endeavour to give us the sense of team and generosity of spirit to conquer the sense of isolation and alienation that divides people and organisations. They engage and work with others towards a common good through the strength of their empathy and competency to listen – a deep consciousness of the other, so to speak.

### Lead

They work well with people, all people, because they know representation matters. They realise that competency in collaboration involves bringing a team of people together in a community of inquiry and practice by building coherent and relational systems and processes that respect all voices. This relies on the capacity to work effectively, responsibly and respectfully for and within diverse teams towards the accomplishment of shared aspirations, goals and learning.

### Work

Their work is grounded in learning about teams. This helps them acquire knowledge of how people live well in community with each other; gain skills that support positive interactions between individuals and groups within a community of inquiry and practice; nurture a disposition towards achieving shared goals for wellness through processes that enhance collective connection and coherence; and build their capacity to reflect on the relational quality of their collaboration.

## Building systems and operations: The purpose of leaders who enrich

Though creating and maintaining teams is critical to the success of leaders who enrich, they also need to develop the capacity to exercise the strategic lever of building systems and operations that habitually and deliberately bring people together to learn, live, lead and work. David Price offers similar insight.

> **GAME CHANGER INSIGHT**
>
> *'There is never a shortage of really interesting learning opportunities within our context. As an educator, you have to think,* How can I design something which will actually benefit our local community and help bring that together?'
>
> — David Price

Thus, leaders who enrich also work to build both relationships and relational systems and operations within an appropriately resourced community of inquiry and practice. They are inspired by a desire to improve the outcomes of their learners, especially in future-fit character, competency and wellness so that they are equipped, empowered and enabled to assume responsibility for making a positive contribution to the world. They encourage habits of researching, identifying and implementing the best possible systems and operations to enhance a relational approach to teaching and learning. They work together with teams to improve what they do as a focused and committed community of inquiry and practice, especially for their students. They prioritise establishing and continuously refining systems and operations that nurture schoolwide, future-focused and evidence-based approaches that unlocks defensive default positions while supporting individual and collective improvement in formal and informal learning culture and practice.

So, team creators build robust and resilient learning relationships within their communities of inquiry and practice. But why are relationships so important in schools? What do we mean by good relationships in schools and what do we need to do to build them? How might we concentrate our efforts on developing the ability of our community to generate relationships that help us attain the fundamental goal of improved outcomes for learners?

At a School for tomorrow. we believe that good relationships should be at the heart of a community's ethos and success. This is because from well-formed and aligned relationships come the engagement, deeper understanding and more consistent growth that characterise more effective learning for both children and adults. By learning, living, leading and working in relationship with each other we draw on the knowledge, skills, dispositions and habits derived from our social and interpersonal connections. This is a process of developing ourselves and others through a team culture marked by its capacity to resolve conflict.

For students and adults alike, we note from our research that this is especially the case when our approach is crafted within the purposeful structures and environment of character apprenticeship. *Character apprenticeship* is the progression, illustrated in figure 7.1, from articulating to reflecting to exploring as a novice, then from modelling to coaching to scaffolding as an expert. It is a strong yet non-judgemental way of explaining how we learn, in a relationship, from an expert who helps us to acquire the adaptive expertise and self-efficacy we need to thrive in the world. The expert should hold authority throughout the relationship, but gradually yield power to the novice who is becoming an expert in their own right.

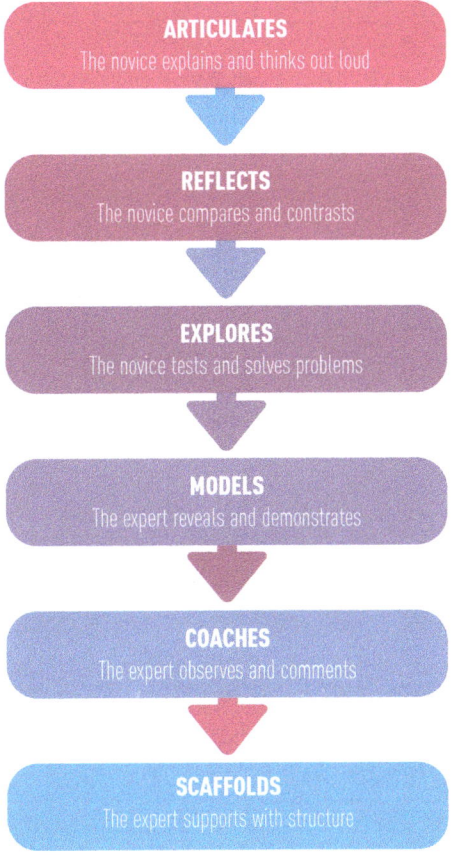

Figure 7.1: Character apprenticeship

The quality of learning in a school is largely the product of specific learning relationships of character apprenticeship in which the character, competency and wellness needed to exemplify the school's graduate outcomes are crafted, and also the way that those relationships bring together all learners in a community of inquiry and practice that is sharply focused on improving delivery of graduate outcomes.

As leaders who enrich, there are further questions we might ask about building relationships with the purpose improving outcomes. How might we use our leadership to optimise authentic and successful relational learning? How can we use strong relationships to promote the healthy dissent and constructive conflict necessary to generate improvement and progress? To what extent can a school community genuinely enact its values within the relationships on which it depends for the success of its work? What then should the expectations be for leaders and team members to grow their capacity to build relationships within a community of inquiry and practice that provides workable and successful answers to questions such as these?

The answers to questions about the purpose and practice of a community of inquiry and practice are most likely to be found within the way teams and their leaders balance the incentive to advance internal culture and the need to meet the needs of the external context of the school – just as the character of individuals is formed in the tension between realising the inner drive to become and replicating the expectations of others. The answers are also informed by enduring values. It's important to note that the way these values manifest is never fixed. Rather, they must follow a trajectory of growth and development that mirrors the way that school culture needs to develop over time to truly serve the needs of graduates, preparing them to thrive in a fast-moving world.

 **ENCOUNTER AND RESPOND**

What defines your character and purpose as a leader who enriches your school community towards transformation through team creation?

# WHERE DO I FIT IN?

## Evaluating enriching leadership

Finally, we will look at the way a leader might measure themselves in their capacity to enrich. Whether you are a team leader or a leader of an organisation, it is important that you know the benchmarks of success.

What, then, are the qualities of leaders who enrich successfully? As articulated in tables 7.1 and 7.2, these qualities hinge on cultivating ethos within the teams we lead and serve.

## Table 7.1: Enriching as a leader of a team

| CULTIVATING ETHOS | Displays a mental attitude of self-belief and confidence in both other individuals and groups. |
|---|---|
| | Provides support to all team members and contributes effectively to high team morale through positive leadership that inspires the team to show high ethical and physical standards of discipline, respect and professionalism informed by values, courage, initiative and teamwork. |
| | Places others before self to influence an ethos of service to the school and its communities as part of a positive team culture that responds appropriately to the school environment. |
| | Identifies potential and actual areas of functional and dysfunctional conflict within the team. |
| | Makes effective choices about methods appropriate to the situation of resolving conflict, brings individuals and groups to short-term agreements and improves long-term working relationships. |

## Table 7.2: Enriching as a leader of an organisation

| CULTIVATING ETHOS | Quickly identifies and understands the school's culture and needs, recognises how its leadership structures work and prioritises issues. |
|---|---|
| | Builds team norms that define expectations of positive and constructive interaction between leadership team members. |
| | Pays serious attention to the leadership team, builds on the strengths of leadership team members and curtails derailing activities. |
| | Models a willingness to seek and accept responsibility, learns and improves, and creates values and value propositions in which fear and jealousy are irrelevant. |

## Cultivating ethos

*Ethos* refers to the way a team or organisation expresses its culture and identity. It is the way individuals see, think and feel together. A leader who enriches must cultivate ethos in order to develop and sustain common sense of purpose; respect for people, place and planet; and shared practices within their team or organisation. Cultivated in this way, a strong ethos will allow a team to honour the new social contract of education within the school context and result in improvement in outcomes that speak to the growth, development and success of learners in how they learn, live, lead and work, and in their readiness to thrive in their world.

To talk about ethos we call on the four central tenets of values and value propositions, vision and vocabulary, morale, and esprit de corps.

### Values and value propositions

As we first explored in Chapter 2 (page 45), values and value propositions are those powerful beliefs that influence behaviour and attitudes towards a shared perspective about what is good, right and important in the lives of the members of the community of inquiry and practice and how this translates into specific and practical benefits for both community members and the community itself.

### Vision and vocabulary

This tenet concerns a statement about the community's preferred future and the implicit and explicit commitment of the community to the process by which it will secure this future for its learners, staff and families. It is supported by a knowledge architecture of words and other symbols that will help the community to form a shared understanding of and commitment to the culture by which vision becomes daily life.

### Morale

Morale is a state of mind, a mental attitude of self-belief and confidence in both other individuals and groups within the community. It expresses the hope, courage and resilience required to embark individually and collectively on the journey of exploration, encounter and discovery that will inevitably lead through at least some adversity to the ultimate realisation of the vision.

## Esprit de corps

The final tenet of ethos pertains to a sense of belonging to and pride in a team and organisation. This esprit de corps is indicative of the discipline of a group that habitually (but not unthinkingly) transcends personal preferences in favour of measuring up to group expectations in their virtues and corresponding actions. It is also built on a shared understanding of the interdependence and reciprocity that supports the individuals that make up the group to be well, make progress in character and competency and succeed in terms of their own inner drive to make their mark in the world.

Leaders who enrich must influence the ethos of the team or organisation and respond appropriately to its environment. They must work hard to ensure group members understand the symbols, artefacts and rituals that comprise the visual identity and events that shape the immediate understanding of what it means to be part of the group. They must encourage individuals to align their own values with the explicit values and underlying assumptions of the group – those largely invisible attitudes, norms and beliefs that have a powerful influence on group members, who will usually find behaviour that contradicts these assumptions to be inconceivable.

They particularly need to recognise that the morale required to endure hardship together is abstract, hard to define and often most noticeable when it is not there. Morale depends on and can be measured by team members' attitudes towards the team, themselves, other people in their organisation, their family and friends, and their leaders. Leaders who enrich by fostering morale do so primarily through their leadership presence, performance and perceived effectiveness. They encourage unity of purpose, shared discipline and self-respect, camaraderie and a good sense of humour (used as a tool to sharpen resolve and robustness, not to denigrate team members or others). They attend to the comfort and wellness of team members and the welfare of their families. They also encourage respect for faith-based and spiritual observance and other customs and practices that speak to a tolerance for culture and background. They foster group traditions and celebrate milestones to encourage esprit de corps, and they are adept at balancing the natural human needs for both competition and collaboration, treating them as mutually supportive qualities when they support performance, the recognition of individual and group accomplishment and identity, and the holistic growth of team and community members within a positive and affirming culture. Zeina Chalich offers insight on this.

> **GAME CHANGER INSIGHT**
>
> *'When people see you not holding judgement and being authentic, that builds credibility and they have trust and confidence in your leadership.'*
>
> Zeina Chalich

Finally, they should aim at all times to balance individual team members' needs with the dominant values of the group and its need to be transformed over time. Being aware that cohesive but rigid team culture and identity may prove a barrier to change, ensure that your culture promotes a strong, cohesive and adaptive team with the flexibility to respond to change. An important way of maintaining team culture is by integrating new members in such a way that they become part of the shared history and experiences of the group. After all, it is this willingness to assist others to become more than who they are right now that is likely to enrich. At the same time, the assurance and depth of experience of the group around them will also add to their experience of the team and its contribution to the world around it. In these ways, positive team culture can accelerate and validate individual team members' attempts to become the best versions of themselves.

No team or school acts in isolation from its environment. Thus, a team's ethos is also affected by the physical, intellectual, spiritual, political, legal, social, community, economic and technological factors of the environment in which that team exists – and these factors are often (at least to a certain extent) beyond the team's control. Leaders who enrich can recognise these limits and their potential to be even more powerful than an expression of internal culture in shaping group norms and expectations. We live in a world that is challenged to be more global in its outlook and more diverse in its composition and perspective than ever before. A diverse environment creates challenges that come with uncertainty. This particular leadership challenge is best met with a combination of foresight, resolve, initiative and teamwork, particularly in the face of conservative attitudes that may promote suspicion of the outsider, fear of the unknown and scepticism of an alternative narrative.

While it is important to watch out for, listen to and act on all complaints received, leaders who enrich understand that the presence of complaints is not an automatic indicator of poor ethos. Life is never perfect; even when the leader, team and community have got the ethos right, people will still have things they need to complain about and may draw attention to legitimate issues that need to be addressed. It is natural and necessary for people to want to vent their feelings about their frustrations and exertions, especially when they are being challenged to improve their performance or struggling to achieve high standards. It is also natural for people to transfer feelings that they have in their private lives onto the team itself.

It's also natural for people to find themselves involved in conflict. Conflict occurs when two parties are unable to agree and so either passively or actively express hostility or interfere with one another's efforts to achieve specific objectives. Conflict is a natural occurrence and can have positive outcomes; some argue that conflict is necessary to produce new ideas and improved performance. Conflict, which we can typically categorise as either functional or dysfunctional, is often caused by change, personal issues and pressures of work. Functional conflict improves the quality of decisions, stimulates creativity, encourages interest and fosters an environment of self-evaluation and change. Dysfunctional conflict, on the other hand, breeds discontent, obstructs communication, reduces team cohesion and threatens group survival. The task of the leader is to ensure that teams undergo functional rather than dysfunctional conflict.

In sorting out the challenge of people and conflict, leaders are often required to intervene before full-blown conflict arises. They will most likely need to gain the support of individuals who are at first unwilling to cooperate. They are usually most successful when they build a team culture of shared values, such as harmony, and then are able to persuade others to their way of thinking. Effective conflict resolution in this instance brings individuals and groups to short-term agreement and improves long-term working relationships. Leaders need to avoid a default approach of conflict avoidance and must instead gain expertise in a range of different conflict resolution techniques. This will allow them to support their teams and team members through difficulty to arrive at positive and constructive sets of agreed outcomes that enhance and align with workable compromises and eventual collaboration rather than destroy and divide through the unilateral assertion of an immovable position. Forcing a hand may sometimes work as a short-term solution, but rarely will any individual lay down completely, grievance unresolved, without seeking at least a process of negotiation. Ultimately, people need to emerge from negotiation feeling that they have gained something that benefits them and with an overall solution to which they can agree, even if it is not perfect. At the same time, people are much more likely to agree to a negotiated solution when they feel as though their feelings have been respected and their grievances have been heard. Sometimes it is just the process of negotiation that helps to soothe conflict.

It is important to observe, before we move on, that the development of a decontextualised ethos – one that exists without serving the needs of people, place and planet in a selfless and disciplined fashion – is dangerous within any team or organisation. It can lead quickly to the establishment of bad culture and superficially attractive but ultimately negative ingrained norms that can take many, many years to change. Likewise, it can be dangerous to build a strong, cohesive and vigorous team or community that has no proper goal to which it can direct its attention and efforts. In particular, teams that do not have positive missions can very quickly develop arrogant, self-serving and antisocial objectives, especially when they adopt having fun as their primary task with no balancing influence of humility, self-sacrifice, responsibility and constructive legacy. This can occur even in a team that appears to have discipline if it lacks positive social values. Preventing the corruption of this understanding is the moral responsibility of all team members, especially the leader. Leaders who intervene when the team is doing the wrong thing sometimes become unpopular because team members often react negatively to being corrected or reminded that their values have been compromised. However, leaders must take a stand, even at the risk of their own standing in the short term. They need to ensure that everyone understands that the moral character to do what is good and right goes hand in hand with the development of a sense of belonging inherent in civic character and the fulfilment of potential in performance character. Leaders who forget this do not win genuine respect from within or outside the team, and negative behaviour from the group will always result in negative consequences.

At the same time, we all enjoy being part of a group that has spirit (what the French call *élan*). Spirit is a risky and exciting thing; it stimulates, provokes, enthrals and, occasionally, leads us astray if we become carried away in the moment. Yet it is part of who we are. We are not solely rational beings – our passions, especially when magnified in a group situation, appeal to a part of us that sometimes needs experience rather than logical thought. Leaders who crush spirit take away something vital from the life of the team. Leaders who redirect wayward spirit achieve much more powerful ends. Leaders who shape team culture and values from the start, who listen carefully to and act on complaints (without always necessarily agreeing with them), and who can redirect energy towards a nobler intent are able to channel spirit towards excellence in every respect. This is why the leadership journey always begins and ends with the values of individuals, teams and the community of inquiry and practice that together comprise a school.

> **(11) ENCOUNTER AND RESPOND**
>
> How might you measure the nature and success of your practice of cultivating ethos in your school as a leader who enriches both your teams and the organisations you serve?

# HOW CAN I BEST SERVE OTHERS?

## Collaborative inquiry: The approach of the leader who enriches

What will enrich us and our colleagues to engage in the vocation of learning as game changers? We know that the work of character, competency and wellness is the whole work of a school; it's the reason why we do school. Perhaps no single phenomenon reflects the positive potential of human nature to grow in character, competency and wellness so much as our very human inquiry into our own motivation. What is it that motivates all of us to be the best versions of ourselves that we can be? In order to grow, each of us needs to focus on our inherent psychological needs. Belonging, the achievement of potential and the need to do good and right things are a very good starting point. But there are others too. We all need a sense of safety and security. We all need to grow. We all need to be loved and wanted. We need to have some fun and we need to express all of the different emotions and feelings that exist within us. We all need to feel a sense of mastery over what we do, we need to feel we have autonomy over our decision-making and processes, and we need to connect everything we do to our sense of purpose in the world. Meeting normal, natural and essential needs like these is what underpins the creation and attainment of every individual's human motivation, the development of their personality and the improvement in their capacity to regulate their own behaviours.

How can we motivate ourselves and our colleagues in education to become engaged, to feel empowered individually and collectively and to identify, adopt and realise a fundamental purpose connected to today's learning for tomorrow's world? If we can understand what makes us as teachers tick, then we can channel our energy and resources in the right direction within a community of inquiry and practice. If this happens, we are much more likely to cultivate the adaptive expertise, self-efficacy, and aligned and dedicated purpose necessary to support the growth of character, competency and wellness for our students. At the same time, we can be more likely to feel as though we are leading a life that's worthwhile and well-lived. Together, in every school, we need to explore the way that the individual growth of teachers and the improvement of outcomes for students can come to define the role and purpose of a motivated community of inquiry and practice in a future-fit school.

We have identified seven successful strategies for planning for and building a community of inquiry and practice with the quantum of character capital required to develop adaptive expertise, professional self-efficacy and instructional leadership among the teaching faculty of a future-fit school:

1. Do it properly.

Use a strategic cycle to establish collective and collegial intent, gather and evaluate data, elicit feedback and conduct intelligence-based planning based on the imperative for both staff competency and student outcomes. Many schools don't do this at all.

2. Work from a knowledge of the staff.

Audit the school's staff (including their learning and working preferences) and work from this knowledge carefully to stretch their capability. Be aware that even in situations of significant cultural transformation, teachers most often privilege a relational and instinctive paradigm that can work against a strategic and performance-driven learning culture.

3. Capture people's hearts.

Plans for improvement will only work when people want to build them and inhabit them. Many teachers just don't like structures that are too rigid and far-reaching, preferring instead to live habitually in a responsive and organic world that overwhelms their sense of personal growth and achievement.

4. Measure what you do.

Beware substituting a feeling or perception about a successfully run event or program for real data about long-term impact on practice and performance. Most schools never measure the impact of professional learning, especially on teacher capability and student learning.

5. Coach for personal and collegial success.

A coaching model really helps to build an environment in which teachers feel safe and can establish high levels of trust in their colleagues and leaders before engaging in constructive risk-taking behaviours that seek to change practice. Existence proofs are essential for mitigating fear and anxiety about change, cynicism about motive and scepticism about what the future really looks like.

6. Consider establishing a centre for amazing things.

Organising professional learning around a centre for 'amazing things' – research, innovation, creativity, professional learning and so on – can be a really effective way to concentrate focus and energy on improving the culture of professional learning. The scope and mandate for this centre needs to be very tightly controlled or else its impact may be diluted. The leadership of the centre should be shared with the school's leadership team.

7. Take the time required.

Building the motivation, determination and capacity of teachers to improve outcomes for students takes time, and tangible improvement will only be visible after at least two to three years. It will then typically take five to six years – or even up to ten to twelve years – of consistent action for that to translate into lasting positive cultural change. Schools that rush these expectations can end up with little significant reform for the investment.

The key to our growth and the quality of the work that we do in improving outcomes for students so often lies in the choices that we make and our disposition towards them. Can we find our inner sense of who we might become (our intrinsic motivation) and balance this with meeting the expectations and approval of others? Can we adopt the ethically sound challenges and opportunities presented by others as our own? Can we balance the competing pressures and develop solutions that feel right to us – a best fit, even if it is a compromise? Can we blend the narratives posed by both intrinsic and extrinsic factors into a compelling story that motivates us to become the professionals we want to be?

We can start by co-constructing a knowledge architecture through which we can track the nature of learning relationships and the impact they have on the attainment of outcomes for the learner, the school and the community. This is why teams need to collaborate to support the community of inquiry and practice as the knowledge engine of school culture. There are a couple of ways to do this. We may collaborate to share our understanding of how this collective knowledge might be applied to progress the learning of groups and individuals for whom differentiation of practice will be required to help their voice, agency and advocacy to emerge over time. We may also collaborate so that we might share with each other what we have learned, testing our assertions against the evidence we have accumulated and the experiences of others.

This is what the real work of teams within the community of inquiry and practice looks like when it tends to the challenge of the learning work. Teams should not be created and perpetuated for the sake of their own identity. They should exist to advance the purpose of the school. If, therefore, there is a model for building a high-performance learning culture among students (one that focuses on a secret sauce that equips, empowers and enables the learning work that results in better outcomes for learners), what might be the specific correlating leadership activity – the leadership work – that creates intentional relationships designed to achieve high performance? What questions might leaders ask about such activity? Let's return to three key components of our purpose to offer the following essential questions about that leadership work:

- Equipping

Are we constructing a contextualised process for change and improvement that equips people with the confidence and influence to function at their best? Are we supporting people with an agreed narrative towards the future and exemplars of success that show how best to embark on this journey?

- Empowering

Are we building commitment to a participatory citizenship focused on empowering people with agency and voice gained through opportunities for experience and reflection?

- Enabling

Are we defining the approach, mapping the route and ensuring an enduring integrity of aligned ethos, strategy, leadership, governance and operations to enable people to grow in the character and competency required to build culture and improve outcomes for students?

We need to accept that as we seek to enact the model of equip–empower–enable in locating our sense of purpose and aligning it to improved outcomes for learners, whatever we choose to do, there will be times of great hardship, frustration and difficulty in our professional lives. For some there may even be more of these than times of great happiness and celebration. There will also be long periods buried in the process of improvement, of doing the many, many repetitions of actions so that they become habits and (in time) genuine competencies. And then we can pass these competencies on to our students!

On this note, Alan Duffy, leading astronomer and professor at the Centre for Astrophysics and Supercomputing at Swinburne University of Technology and lead scientist at the Royal Institution of Australia, reminds us of the value of contribution and the important impact of a legacy of leadership that enriches at personal, tactical, strategic and global levels.

> **GAME CHANGER INSIGHT**
>
> *'That sense of a lasting contribution, however small, is what I do in science. That is the driver behind my efforts. My research is trivial. Next to the giants, next to the greats. But every advance, no matter how small, is an advance. And the body of work builds and humanity advances. And that is something that I feel a great sense of solace and comfort that no matter how small my contribution, I have helped in this species wide effort to know our world, our universe and ourselves better. That's my contribution.'*
>
> — Alan Duffy

In completing this work, we will have freed ourselves from the tyranny of content dot points and embraced, through reflection, a sense of what we really believe and how we might align our practice to a set of beliefs and self-perceptions that we develop in our classes, teams and other activities. These include:

- our sense of who we are, who we are becoming and how we relate to others
- our attitude and how it affects our self-awareness, interest, relevance and curiosity
- the value we place on ourselves, others and the things in which we are engaged
- the values we hold that tell us what the right thing is to do
- our adaptive expertise and self-efficacy, especially our capacity to set and reach our goals.

If we make the right choices about how to engage in our professional lives through these beliefs and self-perceptions, we are much more likely to end up feeling empowered to make that difference in the lives of our students that we want to. We will end up much more invested in what we do and much more likely to see through the difficulties that arise, then build the required content, attain mastery of it and ultimately apply it to how we learn, live, lead and work.

> ## ⓘ ENCOUNTER AND RESPOND
>
> We invite you to encounter and respond to a process of thinking differently about leadership through collaborative inquiry:
>
> - What does using collaborative inquiry as a leader look like in your school? What *should* it look like in your school? Respond by collecting images and keywords, which may also include original drawings and text, that best articulate your vision for high-performance.
>
> - What could it mean to think differently about using collaborative inquiry to lead in your context? What kinds of changes can you make to your leadership practice to support this?

## WHOSE AM I?

Leaders that enrich understand the importance of other-centredness and pass this on to their teams and organisations. They recognise that individuals grow best in community because of their interdependent relationships with those around them and desire to serve their communities from the heart of these relationships. Ultimately, each of us is enriched by the presence and contribution of those around us, and our leadership needs to find ways to bring people together to learn, live, lead, work towards and realise that shared sense of purpose that brings values and value to us all.

**ENCOUNTER AND RESPOND**

Are you a leader who enriches? We invite you to encounter the following reflective questions and respond to them by identifying two to three priorities for your own professional learning and the growth of your adaptive expertise and self-efficacy as a leader who enriches:

- How do I empower others by developing their agency, responsibility and commitment in alignment with my school's vision and strategic direction?
- How do I strive to develop an expert culture of disciplined collaboration for rigorous reflective practice, critical inquiry and planning focused on the achievement of student outcomes?
- How do I ensure the staff evaluation and professional learning practices at my school promote reflection, learning and a commitment to growth within a structured journey from novice to expert, mutual support and dialogue to improve practice?
- How do I monitor and continuously evaluate the quality of culture and relationships in valuing the dignity and worth of every individual, and plan programs and initiatives accordingly?
- How do I value and develop student voice and agency as an important educational outcome on their pathway to excellence?

Our leadership of and with others depends on the success of our capacity to promote a sense of belonging, to recognise and support the processes by which possibility is fulfilled, and to enable that which is good and right in people to come to the fore. If we in schools (and elsewhere, for that matter) can strive together to become the best versions of ourselves, we stand a much better chance of creating today's learning for tomorrow's world. In this way, we all might be enriched by the high-performance learning culture that equips, empowers and enables people to thrive in their world. If we are going to lead with this purpose in mind, then we need to think about how our model of leadership might be constructed and implemented within our communities of inquiry and practice. This is what we will explore in the epilogue to this book.

# EPILOGUE
## The character of game-changing leadership

## WHAT HAVE WE LEARNED?

Towards the start of this book, we asked what it might mean to lead culture, leadership, learning, performance, strategy, and systems and operations in a school for tomorrow and how we might prepare ourselves to do that. We believe that we have answered this question in the chapters since with three central ideas:

1. Our leadership begins with our being – who we are as people right now.
2. It should flow into who we want to become as we seek to guide those in our communities of inquiry and practice to become the best versions of themselves.
3. Finally, it should be demonstrated through our modelling of the character of game changers.

So, what does it mean to be, become and model the character of game changers for others?

### Being game changers

First, let's think about game changing leadership as being. None of us can do the leadership of being on our own – we are all interdependent. Our collective leadership comes from the centre, from the core of our purpose. This core purpose as leaders in schools should reflect, in one way or another, the need to build a community of inquiry and practice that equips students with the character, competencies and wellness needed to thrive in their world.

What is at the core of the process of inquiry, which is in turn at the heart of being game changers, in all of this? In learning about the leadership of game changers in this book, we've asked the four fundamental questions of the inside-out developmental process of leadership formation again and again:

1. Who am I?

This is the question of identity and self-awareness, which is answered through the competency to learn.

2. Where do I fit in?

This is the question of community and relationship, which is answered through the competency to live.

3. How might I best serve others?

This is the question of service and commitment, which is answered through the competency to lead.

4. Whose am I?

This is the question of vocation and calling, which is answered through the competency to work.

We have proposed that leadership is the capacity to influence, inspire, direct and motivate people to achieve a shared sense of purpose willingly. Each of these four key verbs – influence, inspire, direct and motivate – corresponds to the contemporary competencies of learn, live, lead and work that we examined in Chapter 1. The following diagrams can help you to refresh your memory of these competencies.

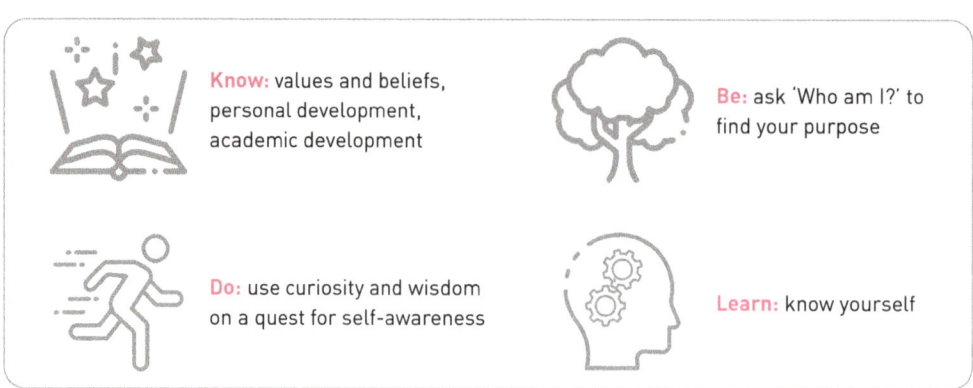

Figure e.1: Grow as you learn

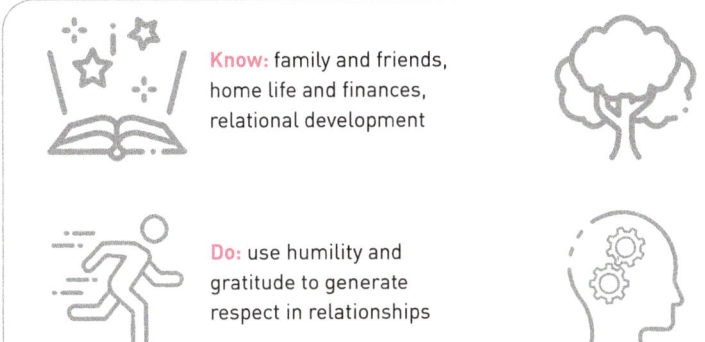

Figure e.2: Grow as you live

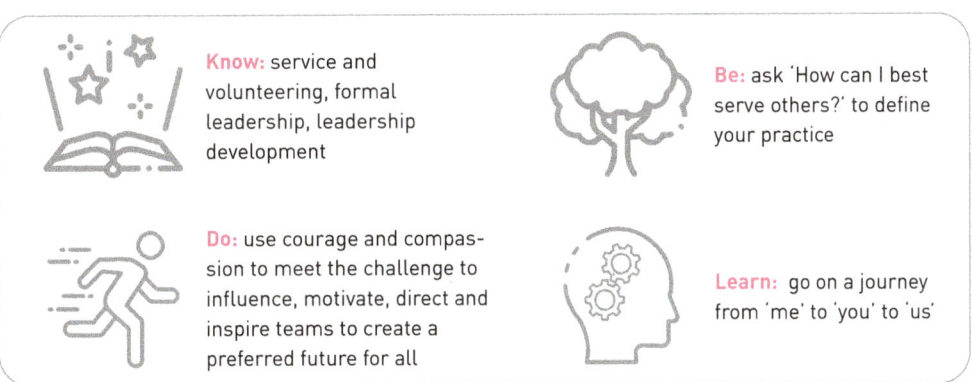

Figure e.3: Grow as you lead

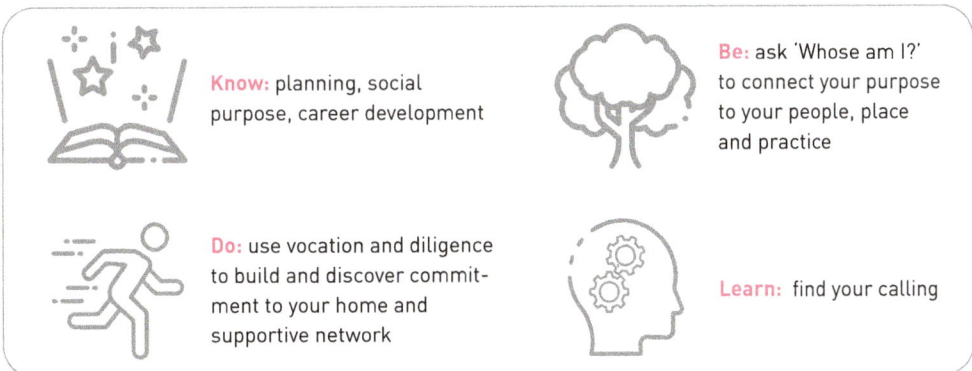

Figure e.4: Grow as you work

We can assist our schools and those in them to become evidence-based and research-driven by answering their questions about how best to prepare students to learn, live, lead and work and how to build out these competencies through the inside-out process of development. This is important support to offer as these communities become increasingly focused on educating future-fit young people with the high-performance character to thrive, all because we have equipped, empowered and enabled them with adaptive expertise and self-efficacy in today's learning for tomorrow's world.

Context is important because all of us are called on in different ways to lead with these goals in mind. Some do this on a grand scale in leadership on a political or corporate scale, while others pursue this in more humble ways through their families and friends and colleagues. For some, leadership is the capacity to influence, inspire, direct and motivate others to achieve what they might not otherwise – to put the interests and goals of the team or group before their own normal, natural and biologically programmed self-interest.

Identifying the role you might have in leading others requires that you first understand yourself and conceive of your context. The inside-out nature of this is critical. Many approaches to teaching leadership work on the exterior first: skills, capabilities and competencies. But it is a bit like working on a house: you can paint the exterior any way you like, but without solid construction and a fitting place within its surroundings, no amount of surface modification can make up for poor architecture. You have to build your leadership from the inside out. This is about building your character and applying it to all of the dimensions of your leadership.

Game changers need to understand the significance of this challenge and how it works its way through school culture from the inside out through the process of becoming.

## Becoming game changers

Now let's think about leadership as becoming. In our world today we demand the best possible education for our children as they become young adults. We want this to unlock a lifetime of possibilities and to create pathways to success for them. We know that our schools strive to help children be thoroughly equipped for entry into the adult world. And yet, as with all human institutions, no school is perfect. Some schools will excel in many areas, while others have a more limited range of excellence. Some communities are very supportive of their schools; in other schools the work of the staff is enhanced by only the core of the community.

What is common to all successful and dynamic learning communities is their capacity to improve what it is that they do – to become the best versions of themselves in the same way that those within schools strive to help others become the best versions of themselves. A school's reputation used to thrive on a steady dose of recall-based learning. Now our students must emerge with sophisticated skills in analysis, synthesis and evaluation, ready to process knowledge in a whole host of ways. The standards of today may be challenging enough for many. Yet, as we have seen, our world demands more and more of us, requiring us to contemplate what it is that students will need in a world where the future is still being co-created.

So, how can schools best approach the perennial task of improvement and convert it into a process of becoming the best versions of themselves? To realise this aim, school improvement needs to flow from insight into and understanding of the school's values and value propositions. We believe that leading as game changers with this insight and understanding can help you to build the relationships at personal, tactical, strategic and global dimensions that assist in achieving the outcomes wanted by both your learners and your school.

We have noted that the leadership of becoming in a fashion that steps forward and up to these external challenges is actualised through deliberate, targeted and intentional action that aligns vision with intention and means. Game changers, of course, are those who do not wait for permission. They are the brave pioneers who can see through to the future, see inside the heart of their community to form a deep intention about taking the big step forward and up to this future, and see their way through to make this happen. They do this despite the challenges and difficulties faced by becoming more proficient in the six key capabilities we explored in Chapters 2–7, recounted in table e.1.

**Table e.1: The leadership capabilities of game changers**

| | |
|---|---|
| **LEADERSHIP THAT STRENGTHENS** | Bringing the values and value of good people through disciplined and purpose-driven practice |
| **LEADERSHIP THAT INFORMS** | Sharing the compelling narrative of future builders through creating and communicating vision |
| **LEADERSHIP THAT ORIENTATES** | Generating the growth of continuous learners and unlearners through understanding and managing change |
| **LEADERSHIP THAT FOCUSES** | Sustaining the direction of solution architects through problem-solving and decision-making |
| **LEADERSHIP THAT ALIGNS** | Connecting the vision, intention and impact of responsible citizens through values-based leadership styles |
| **LEADERSHIP THAT ENRICHES** | Cultivating team creators through locating purpose, people, place and practice |

Yet, our experience with schools around the world suggests that for most there is also a significant gap between what is set out in this book and what most of us actually do when exercising these leadership capabilities in schools. Much of this is rooted in our inability to transcend and transform our own characters. What are these internal challenges to our capacity to lead as a game changer? How might we overcome them so that we might become fully attentive to the encounters we have with ourselves, the people we serve and the lives we lead?

We cannot lead effectively if we are afraid of our inner truths, are resentful of others or have lost our confidence in our capacity to simply be. We become fundamentally paralysed. As we explored in Chapter 2, leadership as game changers who strengthen calls us, as good people, to become assured. Assuredness finds its source in our inner authority. Feeling valued by others is lovely and a wonderful ideal; however, leadership calls us to cultivate and define our own self-worth. Self-talk feeds our own conscious influence and the assuredness that others will feel and recognise in all that we do. Our assuredness should generate enthusiasm and hope in the people we lead. On the other hand, it may also cause those who are not aligned with the cause or the context to allege that we are arrogant and inflexible. We need to counter this with both openness and humility.

We cannot lead effectively if we are not willing to heal and grow from the residue of our past. As we explored in Chapter 3, leadership as game changers who inform calls us, as future builders, to become optimistic. Healing is about attending to our wholeness and looking forward to our future rather than dwelling on the mistakes and breakages of our past. Where these are present in our lives, we need to be prepared to do what is necessary to heal ourselves. This investment in self requires a willingness to attend to the struggle and then bring forth our possibility. Only then can we be truly transparent in all our relationships because we bring no baggage or personal prejudice to encounters and conversations. This is about as honest as we can be, the real substance of our integrity and trustworthiness as leaders. Cynics will view our optimism as fanciful and unrealistic. We need to use both reason and restraint in our language and projections to demonstrate that what we believe is supported by the weight of evidence as well as the trajectory of our times.

We cannot lead unless we are driven by an innate restlessness about how to tend for and even improve what has been given into our care. As we explored in Chapter 4, leadership as game changers who orientate calls us, as continuous learners, to become brave in our readiness to embrace change. As what is ordinary in the course of human activity is being redefined on a daily basis, we are all recognising the compelling social need for children to continue to engage in their learning. Students need to know what they are learning. This relates to aspiration. They need to go on a journey of encounter, connection, challenge and discovery to acquire character and competencies – experience. They need to join us as the co-authors of their narrative of this learning journey – agency. They need to discover their own identity and how best to express it through their learning and relationships – voice. And they need to be provided with the time, support and conditions that will help them to make the most of their learning – resource. This requires us to be more than inheritors of tradition or imitators of the work of others. We need to be prepared to be game changers, true pioneers who show the way forward for others and reinvent education. There will be those who portray this bravery as foolhardiness. We need to show that we have a solid appreciation of the risk associated with change and that the balance of probability supports a disposition towards forward movement, whether cautious or bold.

We cannot lead unless we are prepared to awaken a new level of deep consciousness of our possibility to step forward and up. As we explored in Chapter 5, leadership as game changers who focus calls us, as solution architects, to become grounded in reality and, on occasions, just a little bit prophetic. Education leaders need to equip, empower and enable the development of the sense of belonging, the achievement of collective potential, and the doing of what is good and right within the people we serve by inspiring, supporting and challenging them with aspiration, a sense of kinship and pathways to success. To do this, we need to attend to both the detail and vision of an education for character, competency and wellness. In this, we have a responsibility to act from the core of our being – our groundedness – and to feel compelled to share that sacred voice within us – of prophecy – with those most in need. When we do, we become the conduits for a specific type of wisdom that gives us the power to enter into a world imbued with the possibility of the other. Some voices will cast this combination of groundedness and prophecy as presumptuous, to say the least. We can dispel the negative impact of this by enlisting the support of third-party advocates to speak on our behalf, as well as always resisting the temptation to say 'I told you so' when prediction is proved correct.

We cannot lead effectively if we are not prepared to listen. As we explored in Chapter 6, leadership as game changers who align calls us, as responsible citizens, to become reflective. Reflection requires us to attend to the exercise of deep and constructive listening to the self. It also requires us to develop the presence of mind to hear the other, be connected to the other and respond to the other. This openness to real and raw communication must be active and reflective. This is born of an attitude of generosity of spirit that infuses all of our interactions toward other people and is modelled by our own commitment to listen attentively to and honour the rhythm of our own heartbeats. Moments of quiet often speak loudest to us. Some might point to a tendency to withdraw and become introspective as being aloof and out of touch with the daily experience of others who may claim to hold true moral stewardship of the team or organisation. We need to go out of our way to model the process of taking the space to think, putting our thoughts into action, and evaluating the success of our own work through wide-ranging processes designed to solicit honest feedback and tangible improvement. We then need to work out how to carve out the space and provide the tangible support for others to do the same so reflection becomes a transparent and shared habit of a collective culture – part of 'the way we do things' as opposed to a luxury enjoyed only by the leader.

We cannot lead effectively if we lack authenticity and self-awareness, get caught up in any reticence of others to support our work or have a mindset that is closed to the possibility of the other. As we explored in Chapter 7, leadership as game changers who enrich calls us, as team creators, to become altruistic.

We need to become deeply conscious of the other and embrace the notions of co-creation and reciprocity within a shared vision and process for helping each of us realise the potential of our humanity through our education. By inviting others in, we can be highly collaborative, allowing roles and responsibilities to be fluid and evolving through fluctuating times without compromising the accountability and open communication that ensure the highest standards of performance. This requires us to be vulnerable to both self and the other, as we cannot achieve true success alone. People may see this willingness to become involved in the lives of others as interference or micromanaging. This requires us to show an inclination to respect the agency of others by standing back when appropriate, by quietly and effectively pulling our own weight (and perhaps even more), by standing shoulder to shoulder through both adversity and triumph, by taking more than our fair share of responsibility when times are tough and by deflecting credit to our colleagues when things go well.

How might we develop our leadership capabilities and improve our capacity to overcome our internal challenges through our leadership for character? We have six further suggestions from our global research to flesh out our leadership capability structure.

### Your character matters, so show it

Your leadership character is a way of life developed from the inside out. It begins with belonging. The more we wrestle with forming the civic character of belonging, the more likely we are to demonstrate the performance character that allows us to fulfil our potential. The more we feel we belong and are fulfilling our potential, the more likely we are to show the moral character of doing good and right for people, place and planet. This is how we bring the values and value of good people through the disciplined and purpose-driven practice of leadership that strengthens.

### Tell the story of character and explain its value

As a leader, you have a special responsibility for helping a community tell its story of yesterday, today and tomorrow. It is this story that will provide the 'why' to make real the 'what' and the 'how'. It's how you make clear the benefits of the values and value propositions of your preferred future that will help your community move through the inevitable difficulties of a period of transition and a state of transformation. This is how we share the compelling narrative of future builders through creating and communicating vision with leadership that informs.

### Grow and measure character

For each of us the process of learning character is slightly different. Yet, for all of us the crucible of character formation is most likely to be found in the special and designed relationships of character apprenticeship. It is in these that we develop the consistency of mastery, the quality of autonomy and the agency of purpose through growth in our competencies in particular. Transformation of this nature occurs on a developmental continuum over time. As we learn to articulate, explore and reflect, we grow in capacity for both self-determination and self-assessment. Meanwhile, the authority of our chosen expert declines. In time, we use our voices and advocacy in the world to model, scaffold and coach with the authority of an expert in our own right and in turn, with the capacity to measure and affirm growth, progress, success, achievement and qualification, take on novices to show them the way. This is how we generate the growth of continuous learners and unlearners through understanding and managing change in our lives with leadership that orientates.

### We all need character, so expect it of yourself and others

As we develop mastery of our competencies, we also need to demonstrate the adaptive expertise and self-efficacy that allow us to thrive in the world. We need to be able to build the future by learning and unlearning what we need, designing solutions and creating teams, and becoming good people and responsible citizens. This is the high-performance character that makes us worthy of the challenge of serving others through our vocations as future-fit leaders. This is what will sustain the direction of solution architects through problem-solving and decision-making with leadership that focuses.

### Build a home where character belongs

We have learned that the ecosystems that house today's learning for tomorrow's world must have four particular qualities to grow the future-fit, high-performance character of thriving: they must be human centred; technologically enriched; people, place and planet conscious; and intentionally purposeful. We can use values-based leadership styles to engage and motivate learners, teachers, leaders and school teams to construct such learning ecosystems as communities of inquiry and practice that connect the vision, intention and impact of responsible citizens through leadership that aligns.

### Invest in people through character

If we are going to belong, fulfil our potential and do good and right things in the world, we need to know that we can put our purpose into practice through our engagement with people, place and planet. So much of this is about the hope and love we imbue in how we support the development of the character of those who journey with us. We need to resolve to increase the level of character capital in our teams and organisations: the quantum of future-fit, high-performance character demonstrated in the values and behaviours of individuals and in their relationships with others. This is how we prepare the ground in which we might locate the purpose, people, place and practice and ultimately cultivate team creators with leadership that enriches.

To summarise and a provide a central reference point, in table e.2 (page 190) we have mapped six key understandings about developing your leadership to the capabilities illustrated on page 184.

### Table e.2: The leadership capabilities and development of game changers

| GAME CHANGER CAPABILITY | STEPPING FORWARD AND UP TO EXTERNAL CHALLENGES THROUGH SERVICE AND VOCATION | OVERCOMING INTERNAL CHALLENGES THROUGH GROWTH |
|---|---|---|
| LEADERSHIP THAT STRENGTHENS | Bringing the values and value of good people through disciplined and purpose-driven practice | Becoming assured allows us to show the character that matters |
| LEADERSHIP THAT INFORMS | Sharing the compelling narrative of future builders through creating and communicating vision | Becoming optimistic allows us to tell the story of character and its value |
| LEADERSHIP THAT ORIENTATES | Generating the growth of continuous learners and unlearners through understanding and managing change | Becoming brave allows us to grow and measure our own and others' character |
| LEADERSHIP THAT FOCUSES | Sustaining the direction of solution architects through problem-solving and decision-making | Becoming grounded (and even prophetic) allows us to expect high-performance character of ourselves and others |
| LEADERSHIP THAT ALIGNS | Connecting the vision, intention and impact of responsible citizens through values-based leadership styles | Becoming reflective allows us to build a home where character belongs |
| LEADERSHIP THAT ENRICHES | Cultivating team creators through locating purpose, people, place and practice | Becoming altruistic allows us to invest in people through our character |

## Modelling the character of game changers

We have seen that the leadership of being and becoming is underpinned by leadership for and with character. During this current global pandemic, many individual education leaders and learning communities have encouraged us to rethink what a future-fit education can and should be. While this may have prompted many of us to reflect on the nature of being and becoming a game changer in future-fit schools, how many of us actually have the character required to lead in such circumstances? No doubt many individuals aspire to leadership, take on leadership, and even write about leadership, but do they have the proclivity to look within and outside of themselves to locate an intentional capacity to wake up each day and dream of a new and better tomorrow, and then also to step forward and up to make it happen?

In our work, asking and answering the four questions of the inside-out process of leadership formation is the process of leadership learning that we share with the world. There are any number of ways in which people can project leadership into their surroundings, but unless these are imbued with a critical set of values that run all the way through the leader's being and work, we are left with hollow and meaningless words. There is too much of this in our world today, although we suspect that there has always been a considerable amount of hot air spouted in the name of leadership. The funny thing is that people will forgive leadership that is genuine, but poorly executed; what they will not tolerate is leadership that is disingenuous, cynical and self-serving. They will not accept populism when it lacks the courage of conviction. They are wary of grand words that are not backed up by results.

Those who might follow us seek first evidence of our own character and capacity to lead by example. They want to see a selflessness that corresponds to the concept of *ubuntu* – 'I am because you are' in the Bantu languages of southern Africa – that drives us to see beyond ourselves. This demands that we balance and nurture complexity, rather than simply reduce things to a collection of maxims and seductive simplicities that might be easily taken in at first glance but do not resonate with integrity in response to the challenge of being people of good character.

So, what is this thing called character and how do we lead with it? Some people will talk about character as though it is just one thing, the thing that makes the most sense to them. Perhaps they see it as the thing you do when no-one is looking; yet character is also formed when others are in the room and keenly observant. Perhaps it is the thing that we do in response to adversity; however, what we do in times of bounty and pleasantness says just as much about who we are. Some isolate it to a single quality or competency, such as grit; but imagine a lifetime spent only being gritty!

Character is much more than this. Character is how we live our lives. It is about how we try to find a sense of belonging – our civic character. It is about how we try to fulfil our possibility – our performance character. It is about how we try to do that which is good and right in our lives – our moral character.

And yet we do none of these things completely or perfectly or separately. For most, dealing with imperfection means contemplating either that which we can manage to do or that which we can't. As we talk with people around the world about character it is striking to us how different the approaches of those who see striving and accomplishment are to the approaches of those who see failure and deficit. Some seek motivation in identifying faults and remedying them, while others start by building strengths and develop themselves from there. Rarely do these two methodologies meet in the same person.

The evidence of the world of positive psychology would have us focus on our strengths. Others might encourage us to reflect on our foibles or weaknesses and either attempt to fix them or move around them. Again, attaching ourselves to one or the other approach seems unrealistic and inauthentic for most. Even the most upbeat of go-getters crash from time to time, while the dourest of self-critics allows themselves, on occasion, a moment of quiet self-congratulation. Even the loud and strident can become quiet and contemplative, while the gentle and submissive can find a strong voice and agency.

Nothing to do with character, with the way we live our lives, is as simple as we might want it to be. There is no self-help regime that can provide a quick solution or a perfect answer. Life is suited to neither.

What we have found is that character development is about wrestling – the wrestling between where we were yesterday, where we are today and where we might be tomorrow. It's about our mark as a person (who we feel we might become from the inside) and our measure as a person (how we respond to external expectations). Yet, like Jacob wrestling with the man in Genesis 32, we can't resolve this on our own. No solution ever comes close. As the Yiddish proverb puts it, *mensch tracht und Gott lacht* – 'man plans and God laughs'. Or perhaps we might express it in the fashion of the Miley Cyrus song: 'Things fall apart / Nothing breaks like a heart'.

Even so, we press on. We must press on even when the road ahead is narrow and steep and difficult because we must. We must have hope and we must have love – and we must have the character required to see the journey through.

We want to point you towards the particular character of game changers. This character will help you to clarify what makes your school distinctive and how each member of your community can play a part in bringing about this distinctiveness. It will encourage you to foster champions of uniqueness who will deliver results across the whole of learning in a way that will demonstrate that your shared purpose has been put into practice for the sake of people, place and planet. With the character of game changers, you can embrace the opportunity of being and becoming by supporting all to relate, connect and achieve in a way that will make real the values and value propositions at the heart and soul of your community.

Each chapter in this book is filled with insights from game changers, from across education and industry, who we have had the privilege to feature on our podcast, encountering firsthand their live practice and character essence. You will remember that in Chapter 6 (page 144) we talked about good schools and great schools. Good schools get the fundamentals right, while great schools assemble the secret sauce of high-performance culture. Leaders of character do the same. The fundamentals are those things that we are often told are the key skills for our times – the four Cs: critical thinking, creativity, collaboration and communication. You will have seen us refer to each of these at multiple points throughout this book.

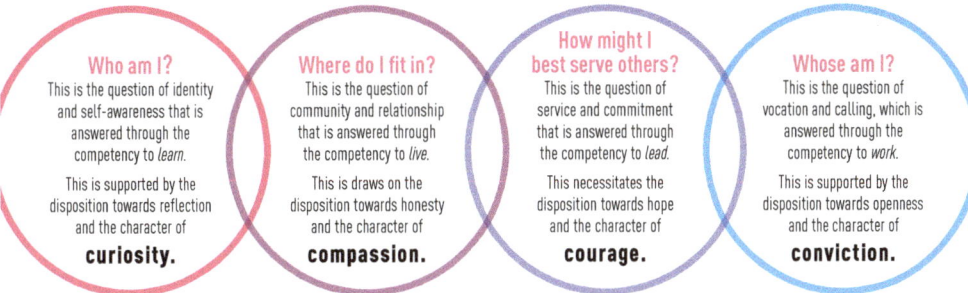

Figure e.5: Four Cs of the character of game-changing leadership

To these we would like to add four new Cs – curiosity, compassion, courage and conviction – shaped by the four questions of the inside-out leadership formation process. We propose that these four Cs, as illustrated in figure e.5, are the secret sauce of the high-performance leadership of game changers. The four Cs are why game changers are able to do what they do. It is how they live their lives through the inside-out developmental process of The Pathway to Excellence – never completely and never perfectly, but inevitably demonstrating the capacity to draw on one or more of their curiosity, compassion, courage and conviction to take the big step forward and up to an extent that others have not yet seen. They can then teach others how to be and become better versions of themselves by asking the four questions that drive all growth in character, competency and wellness:

1. Who am I?
2. Where do I fit in?
3. How can I best serve others?
4. Whose am I?

We should all be able to recognise by now how hard-heartedness and cynicism can defeat the four questions of inside-out development. Real answers to them lie more tangibly in powerful and affirming relationships with others. These relationships, in turn, need to be blessed with the kindnesses of warmth, openness and generosity of spirit. Our relationships with others can't be built around the self-centred (and ultimately self-defeating) pursuit of perfection. In a perfect world, we would all be perfectly formed with everything that we need; we would have no need for each other because we would be complete in and of ourselves. Yet we know we don't live in such a world. All of us are flawed. All of us are broken.

This is why the act of giving is so important. Leonard Cohen's beautiful song 'Anthem' explains it well:

*Ring the bells that still can ring*

*Forget your perfect offering*

*There is a crack, a crack in everything*

*That's how the light gets in.*

When we give to others, we shine a light into the dark crevices of their brokenness. Without brokenness, the light would be deflected and diffused from an impermeable surface. Without imperfection and vulnerability, we could not share in our humanity. We could not console or bring joy. We could not give. The act of giving, therefore, and the quality of kindness that it embodies must be located within the other-centred willingness to give freely and selflessly of our character to others.

It is this other-centredness that might be described as the essential disposition of game changers. If we apply the benefits of transformation through the inside-out process of development only to ourselves, we miss the point that transformation works best when it takes place with others. Giving in to the need to learn and grow allows you to come to know yourself by asking, 'Who am I?' Giving out your gifts and talents allows you to earn your place by asking, 'Where do I fit in?' Giving by going on a journey from me to you to us by asking, 'How can I best serve others?' Giving up control of others allows them to take full responsibility for their own progress and find their calling by asking, 'Whose am I?'

How do we move forward then? What dispositions might we need to adopt to lead for others with the character of game changers? We can look at this through our interactions with people, place and planet across four dimensions.

### Personal leadership: Who am I?

We need to lead with curiosity and a disposition towards reflection.

Emerging leaders should draw on a character leadership built on a deeply ingrained desire for improvement that, when combined with honesty and respect for self and others, elicits a genuine interest in, affection for and celebration of the growth and development of others' character, competency and wellness. The strongly relational (and even compelling) personal qualities of many effective leaders and their determination to set the standard and lead by example drives so much of what we do.

While many senior leaders might wish to spend more time building deep personal relationships with colleagues, the reality is that the greater the responsibility that they take on, unlike when they practised their craft earlier in their careers, the more limited their capacity becomes to create those relationships. It's more effective, therefore, for the majority of relationships outside of immediate executive teams to be built through targeted opportunities for connection and leadership by example that inspire aspiration, motivation and engagement. We need to master the elements of character, competency and wellness that will underpin and help to define outstanding performance in the organisation. We also need to learn to be sufficient and even vulnerable without generating an expectation that we are or need to be perfect.

### Tactical leadership: Where do I fit in?

We need to lead with compassion and a disposition towards honesty.

Emerging leaders should draw on a character leadership that respects the need to be truthful – even and especially when it is unwelcome – while developing a suite of different and authentic character leadership styles that will help them relate, connect and achieve with their teams in a variety of situations. This will help to engender trust, loyalty and responsibility. It will create a willingness to explore selflessness and even self-sacrifice in achieving the purpose of the team and wider organisation. To do this most effectively, we can't be all things to all people. What we can do is learn how to present the best version of ourselves to meet the needs of the team we are leading by making wise and timely decisions, managing risk, and generating and making the most of opportunities to excel while supporting others to do the same.

Senior leaders will have more opportunity to create and interact with a greater number of teams than individuals, but in doing so we probably can only allow ourselves to spend so much time with them before moving on to another group. In such circumstances, our role is to enhance the journey of the team through the commitment of our energy and emotion towards their success, combined with providing the best role-modelling of 'the way we do things here'. This is how we influence the development of an authentic culture (the 'who' and 'when') that will direct creative thinking, sound judgement and patient enthusiasm towards the organisation's desired vision (the 'why'), strategy (the 'how') and goals (the 'what').

### Strategic leadership: How can I best serve others?

We need to lead with courage and a disposition towards hope.

Emerging leaders need to draw on a character leadership that is personally humble, institutionally ambitious and grounded in a realistic appraisal of the ever-present gap between what we might want and what we can have (at least in the short term) in the real world. We need to think about how we might balance the apparently competing demands on our leadership to meet the strategic challenges of our organisations without resorting to either magical or cynical thinking. We need to make astute choices as to how we invest our time by focusing on those things that will make the greatest difference in the long run. We need to be aware that how we show the way forward will determine how successful we can be in investing our own personal commitment and effort, and in multiplying its return through the collective investment and support of the community. We need to think about identifying and demonstrating the values and value propositions that this entails: how we do what is good and right in both abstract and tangible ways. We need to think about how we bring benefit to the lives of those whom our organisations serve.

Senior leaders need to create a vision for the destination of the journey and help the organisations to see that it can be done. We need to align, plan, implement and evaluate what we will do. We need to create an understanding of the value of strategy and culture working hand in hand. We need to paint a picture of success and the trajectory of yesterday, today and tomorrow. We need to show how this will develop (most likely) slowly and iteratively, with occasional big steps forward and up, to ensure the greatest positive impact on commitment, intention, design and results. We need to ascertain what evidence we can draw on to show that the story is unfolding well, especially when predictably unexpected difficulties emerge, when time and resources are tight and when the pressures on people to transform and perform are great.

## Global leadership: Whose am I?

We need to lead with conviction and a disposition towards openness.

To do this well in what our friend and game changer Dr Laurence Wainwright calls TUNA times (that is, times that are turbulent, uncertain, novel and ambiguous), emerging leaders draw on a leadership that is creative and resourceful in learning how to connect their teams with the wider world and develop solutions that optimise their opportunities. They do this by harnessing adaptive expertise and self-efficacy while mitigating the threats posed by the seemingly unrelenting volume, pace and intensity of change. In this context we cannot be or become leaders who are anything other than ourselves – the expression of our character. We must lead from the core of our identity through relationships with others and express our stewardship of our communities as a natural by-product of this connection and commitment. We need to learn to lead ourselves in order to lead others. We also need to build meaningful, sustainable and deep collegial and professional relationships with individuals in our teams and organisations to achieve the breakthroughs needed to transition from being to becoming. We need to transcend the sameness of thinking that condemns us to a status quo that will not serve our students well. We also need to show how this transcendence can liberate us from the three most insidious of tyrannies that hamper honest and true communication about changing the game within teams and organisations:

1. the tyranny of niceness, which prevents rawness, extremes and authenticity
2. the tyranny of false modesty, which prevents leadership and sharing of gifts
3. the tyranny of harmony, which prevents constructive conflict, boldness, risk-taking and innovation.

Senior leaders need to help their organisation understand what it is and what it does, track its journey of being and becoming, define its preferred position within a crowded and interdependent marketplace, and situate itself constructively within the context of its local, regional and global communities by reinforcing both the inner drive and the external stewardship inherent within its sense of belonging, purpose and contribution. In this respect, we need to think about how we might build different and intersecting relationships, and exchange ideas and information to establish common interests within them. We need to negotiate our places in these relationships by demonstrating our willingness to commit to providing a perceived benefit to others as well as ourselves. We will also need to advocate for the values and value propositions of what we offer while we nurture and channel precious assets towards our purpose.

Answering the questions of the inside-out process of formation and development helps us to apply the character of game changers across self-awareness, relationship, service and vocation – the four dimensions of personal, tactical, strategic and global leadership. The first dimension, self-awareness, is not a simply solipsistic exercise. Invoking awareness of both the self and the other, self-awareness is always grounded in location to the situation of others (this relates to relationship, the second dimension), the choice to place others' needs before one's own (service, the third) and the development of a sense of purpose that goes beyond the simple acquisition of resources and becomes a genuine consideration of how one might act to better the condition of all (vocation, the fourth). It is, of course, the final and most important dimension, vocation, that speaks to the essence of purpose and connectedness to something greater than ourselves.

## YOUR MODEL OF LEADERSHIP AS A GAME CHANGER

We have referred throughout this book to the need for all of us to build a model of our own leadership as game changers. A model can help our leadership look forward and up. It can and should be used as a tool for imagining and planning for the future, infusing long-term flexibility, strength and purpose into a school's learning architecture, and helping each young person in our care to find meaning, movement and motivation individually and together through contemplation of something beyond themselves. It can form an overarching way of thinking through and deploying those specific competencies and capabilities of leadership in action that have informed much of the core of this book.

We learn to lead because game changers show us the way. They make clear to us their models and encourage us to go on our own journeys, our own pathways to excellence, to meet the challenge of today's learning for tomorrow's world. Then, they ask that we perform the same functions of developing our own models, co-creating the future and passing on a legacy of character capital, of curiosity, compassion, courage and conviction.

So, what is your model of leadership as a game changer?

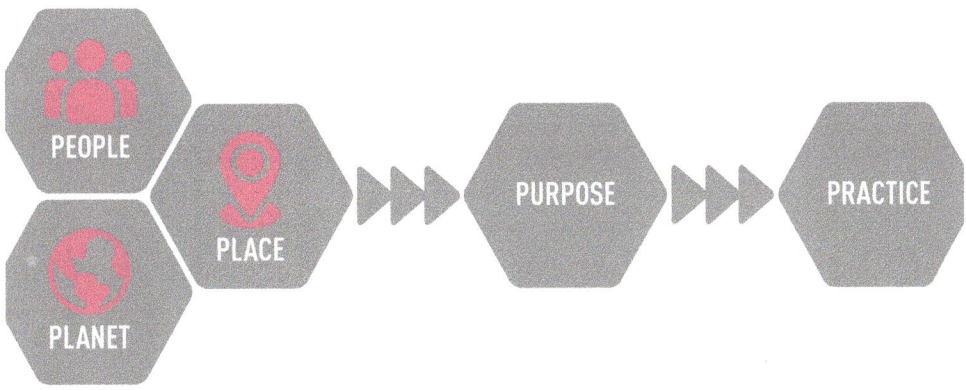

Figure e.6: Model of leadership as a game changer

Please use the following questions and figure e.6 to think about your model of leadership as a game changer:

1. Who are your people?
2. Where is your place?
3. What will be your stewardship of your planet?
4. What is your purpose?
5. How will you put it into practice?

In reading this book you have explored the four questions of the inside-out process and their connection to identity and self-awareness, community and relationship, service and commitment, and vocation and calling. You have seen how these might be put into play with the capabilities required to change the game of school: strengthening, informing, orientating, focusing, aligning and enriching. You have gained adaptive expertise and self-efficacy in contemplating relationships with your communities of inquiry and practice that are personal, tactical, strategic and global. You have thought through how to use all of this character leadership to honour the new social contract of today's learning for tomorrow's world by locating your purpose in your practice through your service to your people, place and planet. You have built your model of leadership. The time has come for you to go out and make that difference you've always wanted to make – to change the game of school.

Life's an adventure – your journey awaits.

Let's go!

# REFERENCES

Bill & Melinda Gates Foundation. (2010). *Learning About Teaching: Initial Findings From the Measures of Effective Teaching Project.* Bill & Melinda Gates Foundation. https://docs.gatesfoundation.org/documents/preliminary-findings-research-paper.pdf

Collins, J. (2001). *Good to Great: Why Some Companies Make the Leap ... and Others Don't.* Harper Business.

Cummins, P. S. A. & Di Prato, A. A. (Hosts). (2020, March 26). Season 1 Episode 1: It takes a village – Stephanie McConnell [Audio podcast episode]. In *Game Changers*. Orbital Productions. https://soundcloud.com/gamechangerspc/stephanie-mcconnell

Cummins, P. S. A. & Di Prato, A. A. (Hosts). (2020, March 26). Season 1 Episode 2: The whole of learning – Yong Zhao [Audio podcast episode]. In *Game Changers*. Orbital Productions. https://soundcloud.com/gamechangerspc/yong-zhao-1

Cummins, P. S. A. & Di Prato, A. A. (Hosts). (2020, March 26). Season 1 Episode 3: Toward a thriving future – Valerie Hannon [Audio podcast episode]. In *Game Changers*. Orbital Productions. https://soundcloud.com/gamechangerspc/valerie-hannon

Cummins, P. S. A. & Di Prato, A. A. (Hosts). (2020, April 1). Season 1 Episode 4: It's all about character – Henry Musoma [Audio podcast episode]. In *Game Changers*. Orbital Productions. https://soundcloud.com/gamechangerspc/gc-4-henry-musoma-its-all-about-character

Cummins, P. S. A. & Di Prato, A. A. (Hosts). (2020, April 8). Season 1 Episode 5: A strong voice and vision – Catherine Misson [Audio podcast episode]. In *Game Changers*. Orbital Productions. https://soundcloud.com/gamechangerspc/gc5-catherine-misson-a-strong-voice-and-vision

Cummins, P. S. A. & Di Prato, A. A. (Hosts). (2020, April 22). Season 1 Episode 7: Empowering young people – Madeleine Grummet [Audio podcast episode]. In *Game Changers*. Orbital Productions. https://soundcloud.com/gamechangerspc/gc7-madeleine-grummet-empowering-young-people

Cummins, P. S. A. & Di Prato, A. A. (Hosts). (2020, April 29). Season 1 Episode 8: Teach your teachers well – Mark Hutchinson [Audio podcast episode]. In *Game Changers*. Orbital Productions. https://soundcloud.com/gamechangerspc/gc8-mark-hutchinson-teach-your-teachers-well

Cummins, P. S. A. & Di Prato, A. A. (Hosts). (2020, May 20). Season 2 Episode 1: Empower through learning – Pernille Ripp [Audio podcast episode]. *In Game Changers*. Orbital Productions. https://soundcloud.com/gamechangerspc/series-2-episode-1-empower-through-learning-pernille-ripp

Cummins, P. S. A. & Di Prato, A. A. (Hosts). (2020, June 3). Season 2 Episode 3: Adapt and iterate – Nikki Kirkup [Audio podcast episode]. In *Game Changers*. Orbital Productions. https://soundcloud.com/gamechangerspc/episode-3-adapt-and-iterate-nikki-kirkup

Cummins, P. S. A. & Di Prato, A. A. (Hosts). (2020, June 10). Season 2 Episode 4: Personal and meaningful – Greg Miller [Audio podcast episode]. In *Game Changers*. Orbital Productions. https://soundcloud.com/gamechangerspc/series-2-episode-4-personal-and-meaningful-greg-miller

Cummins, P. S. A. & Di Prato, A. A. (Hosts). (2020, June 17). Season 2 Episode 5: Think powerfully – Jan Owen AM [Audio podcast episode]. In *Game Changers*. Orbital Productions. https://soundcloud.com/gamechangerspc/series-2-episode-5-think-powerfully-jan-owen-am

Cummins, P. S. A. & Di Prato, A. A. (Hosts). (2020, July 2). Season 2 Episode 7: Transforming teachers – Deborah Netolicky [Audio podcast episode]. In *Game Changers*. Orbital Productions. https://soundcloud.com/gamechangerspc/series-2-episode-7-transforming-teachers-deborah-netolicky

Cummins, P. S. A. & Di Prato, A. A. (Hosts). (2020, August 6). Season 3 Episode 1: Own your story – Vishal Talreja [Audio podcast episode]. In *Game Changers*. Orbital Productions. https://soundcloud.com/gamechangerspc/series-3-episode-1-own-your-story-vishal-talreja

Cummins, P. S. A. & Di Prato, A. A. (Hosts). (2020, August 13). Season 3 Episode 2: Think again – Leslie Medema [Audio podcast episode]. In *Game Changers*. Orbital Productions. https://soundcloud.com/gamechangerspc/series-3-episode-2-think-again-leslie-medema

Cummins, P. S. A. & Di Prato, A. A. (Hosts). (2020, August 13). Season 3 Episode 3: Create your world – Nathan Chisholm [Audio podcast episode]. In *Game Changers*. Orbital Productions. https://soundcloud.com/gamechangerspc/series-3-episode-2-create-your-world-nathan-chisholm

Cummins, P. S. A. & Di Prato, A. A. (Hosts). (2020, August 27). Season 3 Episode 4: Make it happen – Tracey Breese [Audio podcast episode]. In *Game Changers*. Orbital Productions. https://soundcloud.com/gamechangerspc/series-3-episode-4-make-it-happen-tracey-breese

Cummins, P. S. A. & Di Prato, A. A. (Hosts). (2020, September 3). Season 3 Episode 5: Character in action – David Ferguson [Audio podcast episode]. In *Game Changers*. Orbital Productions. https://soundcloud.com/gamechangerspc/series-3-episode-5-character-in-action-david-ferguson

Cummins, P. S. A. & Di Prato, A. A. (Hosts). (2020, September 10). Season 3 Episode 6: Building futures – Debbie Dunwoody [Audio podcast episode]. In *Game Changers*. Orbital Productions. https://soundcloud.com/gamechangerspc/series-3-episode-6-building-futures-debbie-dunwoody

Cummins, P. S. A. & Di Prato, A. A. (Hosts). (2020, September 17). Season 3 Episode 7: Excellence through diversity – Jonathan McIntosh [Audio podcast episode]. In *Game Changers*. Orbital Productions. https://soundcloud.com/gamechangerspc/series-3-episode-7-excellence-through-diversity-jonathan-mcintosh

Cummins, P. S. A. & Di Prato, A. A. (Hosts). (2020, September 24). Season 3 Episode 8: The power of pedagogy – Yasodai Selvakumaran [Audio podcast episode]. In *Game Changers*. Orbital Productions. https://soundcloud.com/gamechangerspc/yasodai

Cummins, P. S. A. & Di Prato, A. A. (Hosts). (2020, October 15). Season 4 Episode 1: Design learning – Cameron Fox [Audio podcast episode]. In *Game Changers*. Orbital Productions. https://soundcloud.com/gamechangerspc/series-4-episode-1-designing-thinkers-cameron-fox

Cummins, P. S. A. & Di Prato, A. A. (Hosts). (2020, November 26). Season 4 Episode 7: Know the game – Zeina Chalich [Audio podcast episode]. In *Game Changers*. Orbital Productions. https://soundcloud.com/gamechangerspc/series-4-episode-7-know-the-game-zeina-chalich

Cummins, P. S. A. & Di Prato, A. A. (Hosts). (2020, December 3). Season 4 Episode 8: Unwavering compassion – Eddie Woo [Audio podcast episode]. In *Game Changers*. Orbital Productions. https://soundcloud.com/gamechangerspc/series-4-episode-8-unwavering-compassion-eddie-woo

Cummins, P. S. A. & Di Prato, A. A. (Hosts). (2021, February 23). Season 5 Episode 1: Redefining learning success – Eric Sheninger [Audio podcast episode]. In *Game Changers*. Orbital Productions. https://soundcloud.com/gamechangerspc/series-5-episode-1-redefining-learning-success-eric-sheninger

Cummins, P. S. A. & Di Prato, A. A. (Hosts). (2021, April 13). Season 5 Episode 8: Doing learning differently – Holly Ransom [Audio podcast episode]. In *Game Changers*. Orbital Productions. https://soundcloud.com/gamechangerspc/series-5-episode-8-doing-learning-differently-holly-ransom

Cummins, P. S. A. & Di Prato, A. A. (Hosts). (2021, May 11). Season 6 Episode 2: Practical innovation – Eleni Kyritsis [Audio podcast episode]. In *Game Changers*. Orbital Productions. https://soundcloud.com/gamechangerspc/series-6-episode-2-practical-innovation-eleni-kyritsis

Cummins, P. S. A. & Di Prato, A. A. (Hosts). (2021, May 18). Season 6 Episode 3: The power of us – David Price [Audio podcast episode]. In *Game Changers*. Orbital Productions. https://soundcloud.com/gamechangerspc/series-6-episode-3-the-power-of-us-david-price

Cummins, P. S. A. & Di Prato, A. A. (Hosts). (2021, May 25). Season 6 Episode 4: Belonging and becoming – Aiko Bethea [Audio podcast episode]. In *Game Changers*. Orbital Productions. https://soundcloud.com/gamechangerspc/series-6-episode-4-belonging-and-becoming-aiko-bethea

Cummins, P. S. A. & Di Prato, A. A. (Hosts). (2021, July 27). Season 7 Episode 2: Iteration, iteration, iteration – Mond Qu [Audio podcast episode]. In *Game Changers*. Orbital Productions. https://soundcloud.com/gamechangerspc/series-7-episode-2-iteration-iteration-iteration-mond-qu

Cummins, P. S. A. & Di Prato, A. A. (Hosts). (2021, November 30). Season 8 Episode 8: Are we alone? – Alan Duffy [Audio podcast episode]. In *Game Changers*. Orbital Productions. https://soundcloud.com/gamechangerspc/series-8-episode-8-are-we-alone-alan-duffy

Dweck, C. S. (2006). *Mindset: The New Psychology of Success.* Random House.

Fullan, M. (2011). *Choosing the Right Drivers for Whole System Reform.* Centre for Strategic Education.

Hannon, V., & Peterson, A. (2021). *Thrive: The Purpose of Schools in a Changing World.* Cambridge University Press.

Maxwell, J. C. (1998). *The 21 Irrefutable Laws of Leadership: Follow Them and People Will Follow You.* Thomas Nelson Publishers.

Pink, D. H. (2009). *Drive: The Surprising Truth About What Motivates Us.* Riverhead Books.

Robinson, K. (2009). *The Element: How Finding Your Passion Changes Everything.* Penguin.

Schleicher, A. (2020, September 15). *Future Proof? Four Scenarios for the Future of Schooling.* OECD Education and Skills Today. https://oecdedutoday.com/future-proof-four-scenarios-future-schooling/

Southworth, G. (2009). *School Leadership: What We Know and What it Means for Schools, Their Leaders and Policy.* Centre for Strategic Education.

UNICEF Data. (2020). *COVID-19 and Children.* https://data.unicef.org/topic/covid-19-and-children/

World Economic Forum. (2020, January 14). *Schools of the Future: Defining New Models of Education for the Fourth Industrial Revolution.* www.weforum.org/reports/schools-of-the-future-defining-new-models-of-education-for-the-fourth-industrial-revolution/

# INDEX

## A
accessible learning, 3
achievement, 28, 56–7
action orientation, 36, 42
action plans, 149
aligning leadership, 22, 43, 131–53, 184, 190
Alphacrucis University College, 2
aspiration, 25–6
autonomy, 104

## B
backwards mapping, 116
Bethea, A, 123–4
Bill & Melinda Gates Foundation, 125
Breese, T, 51, 101–2

## C
calmness, 59–60
Camberwell Girls Grammar School, 61
Centre for Astrophysics and Supercomputing, Swinburne University of Technology, 174
Chalich, Z, 80–1, 167–8
change management, 97–101
character development, 21, 25–7, 32–7, 40–1, 92, 110–15, 134, 163
character of leaders, 47–54, 67–70, 88–91, 112–15, 133–5, 158–61, 187–99
Cherrybrook Technology High School, 159
Chevalier College, 30
Chisholm, N, 49
CIRCLE – The Centre for Innovation, Research, Creativity and Leadership in Education, 4, 22, 46, 116–17
Cohen, L, 194
collaborative learning, 3
Collins, J, 71
communication, fundamentals of, 74–7, 117
compassion, 193

competence, 105

conflict resolution, 169

continuous learning, 29, 86–91, 96, 104–7, 121–2

conviction, 193

courage, 193

COVID-19, 2, 5

creativity, 3

curiosity, 193

curriculum
    evidence-based, 146
    static, 1

Cyrus, M, 192

## D

decision-making, 22, 33, 58, 111, 119–20

delegation, 79–80

disciplined practice, 53–8

disruption, support during, 97–102

Dream a Dream, 58

dress and bearing, 75

Duffy, A, 174–5

Dunwoody, D, 61, 155

## E

*Element, The* (Robinson), 10

Emergent, 94

empowerment, 36

enriching leadership, 22, 43, 155–77, 184, 190

equip-empower-enable model, 144–6, 174

esprit de corps, 167

ethos, cultivating, 165–70

evidence-based framework, 9–10, 38–9, 112–13, 117–18, 146

excellence, 93–4

## F

false modesty, tyranny of, 197

feedback, 80–2

Ferguson, David, 132–3

financial plans, 149

focusing leadership, 22, 43, 109–29, 184, 190

Fox, C, 103

Fullan, M, 42

future focus, 36–7, 40, 70, 72, 85, 117, 120–2, 148

## G

*Game Changers* (podcast; Cummins & Di Prato), 5, 16, 42

global citizenship skills, 3, 55, 99

global leadership, 14

global standards of thriving, 117

good people, 47–50, 52

good schools, 112–13, 125 *see also* great schools

*Good to Great* (Collins), 71

great schools, 28, 36, 92, 129, 136, 144–6, 193

Green School International, 67

Grummet, M, 65–6

## H

Hannon, V, 7, 11, 123
harmony, tyranny of, 197
Havergal College, 22
high-performance
    culture, 28, 40, 116, 133, 145–7, 177
    leaders, 23, 38, 41
    learning, 10, 28, 35, 38–41, 92
*Human Cogs* (podcast; Grummet), 90, 65
human-centred approach, 12, 25, 56
Hunter School of the Performing Arts, 51
Hutchinson, M, 2, 143

## I

inclusive learning, 3, 36
individualised learning, 7, 10
informative leadership, 22, 43, 65–83, 184, 190
innovation skills, 3
inside-out leadership development, 13, 15, 23, 39, 42–3, 46, 66
International Center for Leadership in Education, 110
interpersonal skills, 3

## K

Kirkup, N, 24
Knox School, The, 24
Kurri Kurri High School, 51
Kyritsis, E, 138

## L

Learning Creates Australia, 30
Learning Creatives Consultancy, 80
learning ecosystem, 99
learning hubs, 8
lifelong learning, 3, 29
Lindfield Learning Village, 46
listening, 75
living histories, 126–8

## M

master plans, 149
Maxwell, JC, 15
McConnell, S, 46
McIntosh, J, 68
Medema, L, 67
Miller, G, 30–1, 115–16
Misson, C, 22
morale, 166
motivation, 103–5, 141, 171
Musoma, K, 76–7

## N

Netolicky, D, 38–9
niceness, tyranny of, 197

## O

operational plans, 149
optimism, 60–2
Organisation for Economic Co-operation and Development (OECD), 7–8

orientating leadership, 22, 43, 85–107, 184, 190
outsourcing education, 8
Owen, J, 35

## P

passion, 60–2
Pathway to Excellence, The, 23–5, 31, 33, 39, 72, 83, 134, 193
peers, sharing with, 17
perseverance, 59–60
personalised learning, 3
persuasion, 74, 76–7
Peterson, A, 7
Pink, D, 125
planning, 148–50
*Power of Us, The* (Price), 128
Prahran High School, 49
Price, D, 128, 161–2
problem-based learning, 3
problem-solving, 3, 22, 33, 58, 111, 119–20
Prospect Schools, 68
purpose, 26, 49–52, 70–3, 91–100, 115–18, 136–8, 152, 161–4
purpose-driven practice, 53–8

## Q

Qu, M, 149–50

## R

Ransom, H, 94–5
reflective practice, 16–17, 36, 186
relatedness, 104

relational leadership, 14
relevance, 105
reporting, 76
research-driven practice, 10, 23–4, 146
Ripp, P, 140
Robinson, K, 10
role models, 14–15, 28, 47, 54–5
Royal Institution of Australia, 174

## S

Schleicher, A, 7–8
school for tomorrow, 8–9, 12, 24–5, 36
School for tomorrow., a
    5D approach, 78, 150
    educative purpose, 21
    good relationships, 162
    inside-out leadership development, 46
    mission, 134
    network, 13, 39, 47, 73
    research archive, 34, 38, 41
    research program, 4–5, 25, 30
school strategies, 149
self-awareness, 23–4
self-paced learning, 3
selflessness, 47, 55, 58–9, 191, 194
Selvakumaran, Y, 87
shared model of character work, 26
SheEO, 65
Sheninger, E, 110–11

Southworth, G, 61
St Luke's Catholic College, 30
St Mark's Anglican Community School, 38
staff professional learning, 40
Startmate, 65
strategic leadership, 14, 27–8, 34–6
strategic learning capacity, 35, 37, 94–5
strategic plans, 149–50, 172–4
Strathcona Girls Grammar School, 138
strengthening leadership, 22, 43, 45–63, 184, 190
student-driven learning, 3
style of leadership, 22, 35, 43, 131, 133, 139–42
supervision, 80–2

## T

Talreja, V, 58
teacher agency, 26
teacher voice, 26
team culture, 168, 170
teamwork, 14, 74, 79, 97, 100–2, 155
technology skills, 3, 99
Tecnológico de Monterrey, 76
*Thrive* (Hannon & Peterson), 7, 11
tone, 142
Truman, HS, 119

## U

ubuntu, 191

UNICEF, 5
United Make, 149
University of Kansas, School of Education, 6, 72
University of Melbourne, Graduate School of Education, 6, 72

## V

values, 45–6, 49–50, 56–7, 62, 72, 85, 166
    and value proposition, 8, 11, 45–7, 49, 56, 62–3, 85, 165–166,
VERSO International School, 103
vision statements, 68–9, 79, 166

## W

Wainwright, L, 197
Way, The, 25, 28
wellness, 32–3, 40, 92, 112
Westlake Boys High School, 132
whole education, 40
Wilson, L, 155
Woo, E, 159
World Economic Forum (2020), 3

## Z

Zhao, Y, 6, 72

www.ingramcontent.com/pod-product-compliance
Lightning Source LLC
Chambersburg PA
CBHW051310110526
44590CB00031B/4361